"BIG CY" AND OTHER CHARACTERS:
PAT MACADAM'S CAPE BRETON

BY PAT MACADAM

Cape Breton University Press
Sydney, Nova Scotia

Cape Breton University Press recognizes the support of the Province of Nova Scotia through the Department of Tourism, Culture and Heritage. We are pleased to work in partnership with the Culture Division to develop and promote our cultural resources for all Nova Scotians.

NOVA SCOTIA
Tourism, Culture and Heritage

Cover Design: Cathy MacLean Design, Pleasant Bay, NS
Layout: Gail Jones, Sydney, NS
Printed in Canada by Marquis Book Printing, Montreal.

Library and Archives Canada Cataloguing in Publication

MacAdam, Pat
    Big Cy and other characters : Pat MacAdam's Cape Breton.
ISBN 1-897009-12-7

    1. Cape Breton Island (N.S.)--Biography--Humor. 2. Cape Breton Island (N.S.)--Humor. 3. Canadian wit and humor (English) I. Title.

FC2343.25.A1M33 2006   971.6'90099   C2006-902644-0

Cape Breton University Press
PO Box 5300
Sydney, NS B1P 6L2
Canada

"BIG CY" AND OTHER CHARACTERS: PAT MACADAM'S CAPE BRETON

PAT MACADAM'S CAPE BRETON

EPILOGUE

ABOUT THE AUTHOR

Introduction by Barbara Ann Scott-King, O.C.

Pat MacAdam is a unique man. His talents are extraordinary, his interests varied. As a journalist he is always diligently pursuing the facts. He is an intense researcher and superb writer; some call him "The World's Best Word Mechanic."

He writes in many disciplines – government affairs, sports, business, human interest accounts and events of the world, always with a historian's eye.

Pat MacAdam is a native Cape Bretoner and maintains that heritage with great pride. He has not forgotten his roots and his love of the Maritimes.

You will treasure the book. It is filled with outrageous humour and fascinating, often irreverent, stories.

"Big Cy" is headed for #1 on the best seller list.

B. A. S.

PAT MacAdam is a Glace Bay native and a graduate of St. Anne's High School and St. Francis Xavier University where he earned degrees in Arts and Education. He studied in Carleton University's Master of Public Administration.

His entire working career has been in journalism and politics.

He served Prime Minister John Diefenbaker from 1959-1963 and was Prime Minister Brian Mulroney's closest aide from 1983-1988. He left the Prime Minister's Office to become Minister-Counsellor (Press Officer) at the Canadian High Commission, London.

He was the Senior Writer in the Public Relations Department of the Montreal World Fair from 1963-1967. When Expo 67 closed, he returned to Ottawa as Director of Promotion and Public Relations for Bushnell TV (CJOH-CTV), Ottawa. He produced *Question Period* and The *Judy Lamarsh Ombudsman Show* for CTV.

His articles have appeared in most major Canadian newspapers and magazines such as *Maclean's*, Hudson Bay Company's *Beaver Magazine*, *Cape Bretoner Magazine*, *The Canadian* and *Weekend Magazine*.

He has written or collaborated on three books – *This Firefighter's Life* (2005), *Our Century in Sport* (2001) and *Unbelievable War Stories* (2006). A fourth manuscript, a hockey history of the 1948 RCAF Flyers who won a Gold Medal at the 1948 St. Moritz Olympics, is presently with a publisher. A fifth, a biography of his close friend, Barbara Ann Scott, is nearing completion.

He has written speeches for Prime Ministers, provincial premiers and "dozens of federal and provincial cabinet ministers."

FOREWORDS

By Peter C. Newman

Patrick MacAdam is a born storyteller – not a story inventor or repeater, but the real thing. The pages that follow reek of authenticity. MacAdam's intimate connection with Cape Breton, the very special hearth where he simmered up, gives this collection its tart and true flavour.

Between these covers, his spiritual home comes to life as never before, and that is his very special art. The tales he tells evoke a very special time and place. They give new reality to that storied island: a valuable slice of the Canadian landscape that is rarely remembered and even more seldom blessed.

Nostalgia and loyalty have always been MacAdam's strong suits, not because he worships the past, but because he flourished at a time when loyalty was the dominant virtue, and he practised it in spades.

The last coal mine closed years ago, but Cape Bretoners have always taken adversity in stride – mine closures, fish going south, isolated on Canada's east coast (next stops Newfoundland and Ireland). In a real way, this slim book is a chronicle of survival through good humour in bad times. Patrick's father worked the mines all his life, after his WW I army discharge, as a machinist servicing the huge underground machines that chewed the coal from the face. Fighting for a nickel an hour pay increase was a major uphill battle, and there were many strikes. "During those sometimes bloody disruptions," MacAdam recalls," my father laid in a barrel of herring in brine, a barrel of potatoes and a barrel of apples. That was our daily fare – breakfast and dinner.... I can still hear the continuous wail of the whistle at the pithead – a cave-in, an explosion, or a "bump," when the four walls, floor and ceiling met. It didn't matter where I was – choir rehearsal, altar boy practice, school – the teacher would say "those of you with fathers working underground – GO HOME!"

The several bigger-than-life characters that populate this book were the court jesters who made an intolerable existence bearable by poking fun at the bizarre aspects of daily life. Townspeople took a fatalistic approach to calamity. The miners worked alongside Death five days a week; Friday nights they howled.

Church and family were their focal points. People who had nothing, generously endowed religious charities and gave up their free evenings and weekends to build a magnificent summer camp on the shores of Bras d'Or Lake. Every kid in the parish could go there for two weeks and if a family couldn't afford the $10.00, it was written off. Of course, the most handsome structure on the camp site was the chapel.

Men like "Big Cy" of the title, the fiddlers, pipers and singers staged the often impromptu variety shows in parish halls. Bob MacKenzie's barber shop on Main Street was the local village pump. Even if you didn't need a haircut you dropped in Friday nights to catch up on the gossip.

The noted Canadian critic Robert Fulford defined great stories well told as the literature that matters to us. "They become a bundle in which we wrap truth, hope and dread," he wrote. "Stories are how we explain, how we teach, how we entertain ourselves, and how we often do all three at once. They are the juncture where facts and feelings meet."

This wonderful book is as much about feelings as it is about facts. That is at the root of its emotional clout. It will be make you laugh and cry in equal proportions – and that's the best sign of a great read.

P. C. N.

By Brian McFarlane

Here they are, dear readers. A wonderful collection of the most fascinating stories you'll ever see in print. Chronicled by the amazing Pat MacAdam, Canada's finest raconteur, a man with an abundance of cat-like curiosity, a chap who snoops into the lives of unique Canadians, men and women who were visionaries, ground breakers, heroes and record setters – then writes about them. And how he writes about them!

Like his American counterpart, broadcaster Paul Harvey, MacAdam tells us the story – and the rest of the story. He is a hound dog when it comes to sniffing out the odd and the unusual, the gripping, the comical, the heart warming. He likes to peer into dusty corners, open the scrapbooks and the diaries, and surprise us by writing about subject matter never before seen in print.

One stunning revelation was his discovery that an American president, Chester Arthur (1881-1885), was born in Canada and therefore was *ineligible* to hold the presidency. After lengthy research, MacAdam gathered solid evidence that Arthur assumed the identity of his dead infant brother, who was born in Vermont.

He's the same MacAdam who reports in this book that hockey Hall of Fame broadcaster Danny Gallivan was possibly the finest baseball pitcher to come out of Nova Scotia. Did you know that the famous Maritime giant, Angus McAskill, at seven feet nine inches, had to look up to his spouse who towered over him at eight feet? Or that Johnny Miles from Florence, Cape Breton – the unknown marathoner – captured the Boston Marathon in record time in 1926. The nineteen-year-old wore a pair of 98¢ running shoes! His mark lasted for twenty years.

Enjoy practical jokes? Mac writes about Halloween pranks and how kids in his day would physically move an outdoor privy five or six feet back from its original location.

And how a late night visitor hurrying down the familiar path to the outhouse would suddenly plummet into the gaping hole. His cry of "Holy s…" could no doubt be heard for miles.

These are a just a few of the gems that await you in the pages ahead. Oh my, this is a fun book. Well done, Mac.

B. M.

THE SENATOR OF SENATOR'S CORNER
WILLIAM MACDONALD

Senator's Corner, Glace Bay's best-known piece of real estate, was named after "Senator Mac" (or Mc), or "Senator Billy."

And why not?
Senator William McDonald owned the triangular intersection of Main, Union and Commercial streets as well as dozens of other pieces of revenue property in the town and county.

Senator Billy's holdings included houses and commercial buildings on Minto, York, Reserve and Union streets and Number Four Road, and land on Caribou Marsh Road, Grand Lake Road, Dutch Road, Mira Road and in Birch Grove and Ben Eoin.

If, as bankers claim, money doubles every seven years, his real estate portfolio would be worth millions today.

His father, Allan, emigrated to Cape Breton from South Uist, Inverness shire,

Scotland in 1826. His mother, Mary McDonald, from Stollegarry, Barra, Scotland, arrived in Cape Breton in 1829.

William was born at River Denys Road in 1837. At the age of sixteen he was licensed to teach school and, for two years, taught in the school he had attended. Then he studied at St. Francis Xavier College in Antigonish and taught school for another four years.

Teachers were poorly paid so he moved to Glace Bay and opened a general store, which was very successful. In 1865 he married Catherine McDonald of East Bay. They had seven children. A daughter, Agnes, died in infancy. They adopted a cousin, Agnes Claire, when she was a little girl.

He was a member of the "General Sessions of the Peace" as the representative of Cape Breton County and played a prominent role in the administration of municipal affairs. For years, he was the operator for the Western Union Telegraph Company. He was appointed postmaster of Little Glace Bay, a position he resigned in 1872 to contest Cape Breton as a Conservative candidate for Parliament.

He won four consecutive elections in the dual riding between 1872 and 1882. In 1874, the Pacific Scandal unhorsed Conservative incumbents and candidates by the dozens. William McDonald and Sir Charles Tupper were the only Conservatives elected in Nova Scotia.

In the House of Commons he was, for several years, Chairman of the Committee on Colonization and Immigration. He also pressed for and secured the very first subsidy for the extension of the Intercolonial Railway across the island of Cape Breton.

In 1878, he was re-elected with the largest majority accorded any candidate throughout the entire Dominion.

Family documents indicate he was on the short list to succeed Tupper as Nova Scotia's cabinet minister. A Montreal newspaper (*La Minerve*) of April 11, 1883, described him as "one of the most distinguished members of the parliamentary representation from the Maritime Provinces and, as a member of the cabinet, would be the right man in the right place."

Sir John A. Macdonald offered him the positions of Governor of the Northwest Territories or Governor of Manitoba. He declined both appointments, but accepted a summons to the Senate where he served for 32 years, from 1884 until his death in 1916.

The *Toronto Mail* wrote, "The Commons will lose a modest, useful, unstained and most faithful man. He might have been the perpetual member for Cape Breton, so confident were the people in his integrity and so consistent and honourable was his conduct."

A daughter, Teresa, entered the Sisters of Charity Order, Mount St. Vincent, as Sister Mary Aquinas and became Mother Superior of Mount St. Joseph's Academy, North Sydney.

Two other daughters, Catherine and Mary E. "Minnie," were spinsters living at home with their mother and bachelor brother, Bill, at 755 George Street, Sydney.

Catherine and Minnie travelled a great deal. They had a chauffeur named Gordon who was never allowed to smoke. Unknown to the two sisters in the back seat, he chewed tobacco and "was able to spit casually and expertly out the window when necessary."

On one occasion, he was instructed to close the car window and he had to swallow tobacco juice, "getting sicker all the time."

In a letter to his California cousin, 77-year old Bill Norin, the late Bob Morley of Cumberland, BC, wrote that he was a regular visitor to 755 George Street when he was 5-7 years old. "There was a fourth occupant called only Little Bill – a pale blond boy who was a few years older than I and spent most of his days in bed."

"I suspect that the family wanted to hide him," Mr. Norin wrote.

"Minnie and Catherine always brought me over to play with him. We sat on the edge of his bed and played with his little lead toy soldiers. He had entire armies of them dressed in army garb of the 1800s and earlier.

"I was never advised who exactly he belonged to."

BILLY jr. was an avid gardener and reeked of foul smelling cigars. He cultivated two acres of flowers.

Bob Morley recalled "he did not appear to have any particular occupation or trade, but he was a keen reader with probably the largest private library in Nova Scotia. He was an eccentric, but friendly type. If he was eccentric, his sisters were totally out in left field."

In fact, William Jr. was an accountant and teller in the Glace Bay branch of the Union Bank of Halifax. Senator Billy named him one of the Executors of his Will.

Young Bill's own Will bequeathed $10,000 to his cousin Theresa MacDonald and $10,000 towards a $30,000 memorial fund for his deceased sister, Sister Mary Aquinas. Catherine and Minnie each contributed $10,000 to make up the balance.

Bill left a third of his estate to each of his two sisters and the remaining third to St. FX for the construction of buildings at Xavier Junior College, Sydney. The Executor of his Will was Reverend Dr. Malcolm MacLellan, Principal of Xavier Junior College.

Another son, Allan, had a law degree from Dalhousie and Bob Morley wrote: "I am not sure if he really had a practice."

Allan dressed like a British "toff," or dandy. He lived off his father's wealth. He was the stereotype of a remittance man, but he never left Cape Breton. Instead, he brought England to Sydney. He built a replica of an English cottage and had a thatched roof shipped over from England. Senator Billy left him land on Union Street in Glace Bay.

Bob Morley wrote: "A. J. also had a chauffeur, but the principal reason for that was because he was generally drunk."

Another son, Daniel, also a bachelor, owned and operated a pharmacy on the north side of Main Street in Glace Bay. When he died he excused all his debtors.

Senator Billy had three Wills drawn up – October 1909, October 1913 and July 1915 – with very few variances.

"Minnie" was left nothing by her father.

The Senator's name was spelled both "Mc" and "Mac" in various official publications and parliamentary guides.

However, he signed all three Wills "McDonald."

Except for small specific bequests, he left everything – property, furniture and rental income – to his wife, Catherine.

Senator Billy requested that he be buried in a Catholic cemetery in Sydney and was laid to rest in Holy Cross Cemetery.

In the first and second Wills, he left $120 yearly to Sister Mary Aquinas. This bequest was voided in the third Will, when he left her a lump sum of $2,000. He left $1,000 to St. FX and in his final Will he earmarked $500 to be distributed among the priests of the diocese for Masses "for the repose of my Soul."

Prime Minister Robert Borden sent a telegram of condolence: "Pray accept and convey to the members of your family, our deepest sympathy in the loss of your husband, who gave so many years of useful service to his country."

Senator Billy's funeral Mass was held at St. Anne's, Glace Bay. After a Requiem High Mass, the casket was taken to a Sydney and Louisburg Railway crossing where a special train was waiting to take the remains to Sydney.

The Toronto Mail wrote that he "has never been an obtrusive public man; but when he spoke he was listened to with respect due to one who only entered a debate for the purpose of contributing special information.

"His appointment [to the Senate] especially pleasing to those Highland Catholics who, in common with their friendly allies in politics, the Scottish Presbyterians of the county, have united, on purely political lines, to carry again and again their honourable representative to the head of the poll."

CANADA'S WILL ROGERS
"BIG CY" MACDONALD

Unlike American comic Will Rogers, he never appeared on a stage twirling a lariat and cracking wise. He probably never appeared on stage before a paying audience. Big-time booking agents didn't notice small town comics who didn't play the "Borscht Belt" in New York's Catskills or big city vaudeville houses.

Will Rogers's peer walked among us and we neither recognized him nor appreciated his outrageous wit while he lived.

Maclean's magazine, March 15, 1954, described him as Glace Bay's "biggest booster."

The late Judge Leo McIntyre was Boswell to his Doctor Johnson, but left little in the way of a written record of this extraordinary comic. Judge McIntyre's after-dinner speeches are larded with crib notes that are largely subject headings and

shorthand reminders to himself of stories and one-liners that were not his own.

Most who knew "Big Cy" well are dead. What little remains of him are stories passed on by word of mouth. The Beaton Institute, Cape Breton's repository of local history, has no files or records – not even an obituary.

HECTOR "Big Cy" MacDonald was a hobo, a logging camp cook, a fight trainer and corner man and a bootlegger, but above all, he was a natural raconteur and an exceptional entertainer.

He rode the rods across North America. He lived in hobo jungles. Once, he showed former Cape Breton County Councillor Donald MacIsaac his embossed membership card in the American Association of Hobos.

He is immortalized in a Woody Guthrie folksong as "Cy, the 'bo from the Bay."

Maclean's quotes him: "I've been everywhere. And, let me tell you, byes, as one of God's chosen people – a MacDonald – they's not a place in this world can touch the Bay."

He could be found most summer evenings on Senator's Corner in Glace Bay, regaling his listeners with stories of his days as a "boxcar tourist" – a hobo.

He would rattle off rib-splitting yarns about Fry Pan Jack, El Paso Kid, Hard Rock and Steam Train – other knights of the road who shared "three-bean soup" with him.

Big Cy spent time in New York and ran errands for Eddie Cantor and Jimmy Durante. In later years, two "Bay Byes" were in New York and dropped into Jack Dempsey's restaurant, hoping they might meet the former heavyweight boxing champ.

They not only met him; he gave them his autograph.

As they parted, Dempsey said: "Glace Bay, eh? When you get back home, say hello to Big Cy for me."

THE "CY" MacDonalds came from Catalone—not far from Louisbourg. Big Cy's niece, Lorraine Abbott, remembers a photograph of the four "Cy" brothers who went off to fight in WW I. Two came back—Hector "Big Cy" and Lorraine's father, Jack "Cy."

Fig. 1. "Big Cy" and the boys were known to turn the odd card at Iggy MacIntyre's bar on Lower Main Street, Glace Bay. Front row: "Big Cy" MacDonald and Jack MacRae's business manager Louis Gefter. Back row: Louis Goldman, Harry Smith from Howie Centre and Iggy MacIntyre. Photographer unknown. Courtesy Raymond and Solly Goldman.

Jack Cy had gone to work in the coal pit when he was only nine. Lorraine Abbott's son, Pat, is known locally as Pat Cy.

Big Cy never held a steady job. He lived by his wits and his wit. He bootlegged coal and he bootlegged moonshine. Big Cy never ran a still, but he sold the finished product to regular customers on Senator's Corner.

Locals recall that if you saw Big Cy on the Corner and he was wearing a trench coat you knew he had bottles of 'shine hanging from strings attached to a harness around his waist.

Big Cy was a giant of a man. Bill "Mutt" Kavluk, a former Glace Bay policeman who now lives in Markham, Ontario, remembers that Big Cy wore size 56 jackets.

He was Mutt's corner man when he was an amateur boxer in the early 1950s. He remembers being told: "don't worry about dem guys wit' Sunday punches. Dey never trows dem on weekdays."

Big Cy was in Mutt's corner for a fight in Montreal. His advice: "feel out this tomada and if you see an opening, take it."

Mutt was more than holding his own, Big Cy continued, and "doin' all right when he saw an opening. Well, he hit this fella with a right hand that had a piece of Flint Island tied to it. He knocked him colder than Mahatma Gandhi going to Alaska."

Mutt also remembers Big Cy sitting on his veranda, chewing MacDonald's Twist tobacco and reading The Hobo News.

Fig. 2. Big Cy was in demand as a bartender, mostly because of his quick wit and his outrageous zingers, not just for his pouring skills – although he poured "stiff ones." Photographer unknown. Courtesy "Mutt" Kavluk.

"Want to come for a walk with me, Cy?"

"Nah, not just yet, Mutt. I got two more miles left in this chew."

Big Cy's ring career dated back to 1922 and Mickey MacIntyre, the finest boxer Cape Breton ever produced (page 96). MacIntyre was lightweight and welterweight champion of Eastern Canada. He fought and defeated world champion Oscar "Battling" Matthew Nelson (1882-1954) in a non-title bout in Edmonton.

Fight promoters sent one rail ticket to MacIntyre's camp – Mickey travelled by train and "Big Cy" hitchhiked. When

Mickey arrived in Edmonton, Big Cy was waiting for him on the station platform.

Big Cy picked potatoes on Prince Edward Island.

He rode the "Harvest Trains" out west for the grain harvest.

He was a popular cook in lumber camps and kids' summer camps.

He was a lifelong Tory and boasted that he once sold a newspaper to John Diefenbaker. In 1956, the newly-elected Stanfield government gave him a patronage job in the Nova Scotia legislature. When someone asked him what he did, he said he didn't know. He was a highly paid pageboy-cum-messenger.

Senator Lowell Murray recalls that Attorney General Dick Donohue told him they had to send Big Cy home to Glace Bay because "he was too high profile and the Liberals were asking embarrassing questions about his duties and his salary."

Big Cy was a natural emcee and storyteller. When the guest speaker failed to show for a Rotary Club of Glace Bay luncheon, the organizers were in a terminal state of panic. Someone said: "Go down to the Corner and get Big Cy to be our speaker." After lunch, there was unanimous agreement: "it was the funniest and best speech they had ever heard."

Mutt Kavluk and the late Al Hogan, of New Waterford, invited Big Cy to Toronto in 1966 for Maritimes Night. A newspaper reported he "knocked them dead."

Big Cy would tell tourists and returning expatriates that Glace Bay was unique. Not only the largest town in Canada, among mining towns it was unique.

"Yes, Glace Bay is unique. The word "unique" is from the Latin – *unus* meaning one and *equus* meaning horse."

Then he would point across the Corner to a wooden frame house that had been converted for commercial use. The ground floor was occupied by a funeral home and upstairs by the provincial social services department.

"Ah, yes, there is Glace Bay's only dual-purpose facility. Upstairs is welfare and downstairs is farewell."

One day, undertaker Charlie Curry summoned Big Cy from his command post on Senator's Corner. He invited him into an embalming room to view the spectacular sight of a corpse who was the most generously endowed male Charlie had ever seen.

"Have you ever in your life witnessed anything like it, Cy?"

"Yes, Charlie, I have."

"On whom?"

"On meself," replied Cy.

"My God, Cy, don't tell me you're that well hung?"

"No, Charlie, bye, that dead."

BIG CY was just being Big Cy. He didn't have the guile to be anyone or anything else. He could keep a straight face when he'd tell someone he always thought that roadside JESUS SAVES billboards were advertisements for credit unions.

Cy said he knew "a guy who put a classified ad in the Sydney *Post-Record* for a set of encyclopedias."

The ad read: "For sale. Complete set. *Encyclopedia Britannica*. Never used. Wife knows everything. Phone…."

He'd tell his rapt listeners that "an Upper Canadian newspaper" carried a news

Fig. 3. A lifelong Tory, Big Cy squires Tory party leadership candidate John Diefenbaker into Knox Hall in 1956. Photographer unknown. Courtesy "Mutt" Kavluk.

story about a major fire in Glace Bay. The head on the story was:

> Major pool room
> fire in Glace Bay:
> 500 homeless

THEN, he'd shift gears smoothly. He'd relate the story of a retired coal miner who married for the first time at age 75 and fathered a child.

"Yes, it was Glace Bay's very first case of in vino fertilization."

One of his stock-in-trade yarns was about his dog: "Yessss, we had a dog that was so smart it was a machinist."

A machinist?

"Yesss, if you gave it a kick in the arse it would make a bolt for the door."

Then, he'd segue smoothly into the story of the miner who fell behind in his payments to a local finance company.

"Yessss, they came to his house while the family was eating dinner. They seized the food off the table, the dishes, the table cloth, the table and chairs and, on the way out, they shot the dog."

"Them American and Upper Canadian tourists think we're dumb. They think Cape Breton is Dogpatch. Did you know that last year 10,000 of them came down here to see the Seven Mile Bridge?" The Seven Mile Bridge is about 75 feet across a small brook seven miles from Sydney.

In the 1940s, Big Cy and a chum set out to ride the rods to Boston to see their beloved Red Sox play in the World Series.

"A railway 'bull' caught us at the very first stop, gave us a boot in the arse and kicked us off the train," Big Cy would say. "We got back on and got caught about nine more times before we reached the Strait of Canso. Always, it was the same, a boot in the arse and off the train.

"When we got to the Strait the train was uncoupled and shunted on the train ferry. The railway 'bull' saw us again. Either his foot was getting sore or he was impressed by our determination.

"He said: 'where the Hell are youse guys going anyway'? I looked him straight in the eye and I said: 'Bye, we're going to the World Series in Boston if our arses hold out'."

Without pausing for breath, he moved on to the story about the miner who was picked up by a female con artist in a tavern. She invited him back to her place for some horizontal folk-dancing.

On the way, she told him she had to pick up some booze and groceries. He ended up paying for three 40-ouncers of rum, gin and rye and a huge box of groceries.

They were only in her house for a few minutes when they heard a thump.

"It's me husband coming home early."

The miner fled through a rear window.

Big Cy said the mark told him later: "I wish I could get back there. I left me teeth on the kitchen table."

"Cy" went home one evening and "my supper was in the warming closet on the stove. The wife had gone to the Miners' Forum for the 'rassling matches'."

How did he know she was at the Forum?

"I knew because all the carpet tacks and thumb tacks in the house were gone!"

Big Cy was always dressed to the nines – freshly starched white shirts and bow ties. During summers he was resplendent in a powder blue Panama suit and straw boater.

His daily trap line began at Willie Yee's Broadway Café. Big Cy's office was a corner booth. Willie kept him in complimentary scalding hot tea all day long. Next, he was off to swap gossip with tailor Hughie MacIntyre and then on to Woolworth's lunch counter to chat with his friend, the store manager.

Perched on a stool at Woolworth's, he paid a left handed compliment to an acquaintance: "He is a great guy – delightfully weak."

One morning, Hughie MacIntyre asked Cy to "mind the store for a few minutes" while he went to the bank to make a deposit. While Hughie was away, a grieving widow came in to buy a suit to lay out her husband in his coffin. He had been killed in a mine "bump."

Big Cy sold her a suit with two pairs of pants.

By then it was time to go home for lunch.

He was extremely popular with Glace Bay's small Chinese community. He helped them with correspondence and, along the way, picked up a smattering of Mandarin Chinese. When he travelled he had letters of introduction from the owners of Glace Bay's Broadway, Glory and New Era restaurants. He ate free Chinese meals when he was on the road.

Cy always said he was "growing old reluctantly."

His great heart gave out when he was 82. His trademark straw boater was on his chest when Charlie Curry closed the coffin lid on his old friend.

THE DOMINIE OF NORTHSIDE EAST BAY

PAUL MORRISON

Years ago, *Reader's Digest* carried a monthly feature: "My Most Unforgettable Character." I have met presidents, prime ministers, prelates and pro athletes. They are all unforgettable, but Paul Morrison, a bachelor Cape Breton Scot, stands above the crowd.

Paul didn't hold the Order of Canada. There were no honorary initials after his name. He was comfortable in his own skin and he enriched the life of every person he touched. He was a huge success as a human being.

Paul was, as Scots say, "full of the devil."

He was the "dominie" (an elder) of the northside of East Bay. Neighbours and friends sought his counsel. Lawyers and surveyors consulted him because he knew every corner of his ancestral acreage, where property lines began and ended.

One day, a know-it-all, wet-behind-the-ears bureaucrat looked down his nose and asked haughtily: "You have lived your entire life in Island View, Mr. Morrison?"

Paul's mischievous answer was: "No, not yet!"

One had to get up early to get ahead of Paul. Although he had only Grade 6 schooling, he had the native intelligence, wit and cunning earned only in a school of hard knocks, and he graduated with honours.

He was an institution.

He lived most of his life along the highway, just a few feet from a Bras d'Or Lake.

He was born in 1899 on the mountain side of the highway. When he broke an ankle and couldn't negotiate the steep driveway, he moved down to a small cabin along the water side of the highway and never moved back.

On a clear day he could look across the lake at Ben Eoin and Big Pond – Rita MacNeil country.

The cabin had no indoor plumbing or running water. A two-holer outhouse and septic tank were located out back. His well yielded hard water that was sulphurous to smell and taste. A wood burning stove took up a quarter of his kitchen. The heat it threw off could melt an iceberg.

Paul's Boston nieces, Tootsie Gillis and Terry McAdam, spent six weeks every summer next door to Paul's and they pestered him so much that he installed an indoor toilet. One evening, sitting down to a barbecue, Paul remarked: "Jaysus, when I was little, we used to cook in the house and go to the bathroom outside. Now, we are eating outside and going to the toilet in the house."

His kitchen was *the* local social centre. Friends congregated to play cards – forty-fives – and to smack their lips over one (or two or more) of Paul's "hot ones," hot toddies concocted with moonshine. Paul was a serious student of' shine. He maintained that the best stills were in Frenchvale.

He eked out a marginal living as a road foreman. As a foreman in 1953, he was paid 80¢ an hour; his crew of 10 labourers each earned 70¢ an hour. A timesheet found after his death revealed that he worked nine hours a day for 10 days in March, 1953. His take home pay was $57.60. He also had a small market garden and sold fresh produce and dairy products door-to-door in Sydney.

Paul had a quiver-full of stories about his days as a highways foreman. I heard him relate the story of an over-bearing, rude, tyrannical area highways overseer named Crawley. Two local hourly-rate employees were charged with tearing down an old wooden plank bridge across a small stream.

They chose the lazy man's way. They prepared to dynamite the rotting structure. Just as they lit the fuse, Crawley appeared out of nowhere and walked out to the middle of the bridge.

"Fly to your Jesus off that bridge," the men yelled.

Crawley eye-balled the pair with an icy stare and asked: "Do you know who I am? I am Crawley."

The reply: "Well you'd better crawley off that Jesus bridge because she is going to blow any second."

Paul had another old friend who found work at Beinn Breagh, Alexander Graham Bell's Baddeck estate. Paul asked him if he saw Mr. Bell often.

"Yessss, I saw him just about every day in his workshop."

"Were you in awe of the great man?"

"Paul, I was so scar't of him I stayed still because I feared I'd fart."

AS HE morphed into old age, Paul's slight frame began to shrink and he took on the appearance of an elfin garden gnome.

He befriended some American hunters – PhDs from Massachusetts Institute of Technology who always stopped by for a "hot one." When Paul went to Boston to visit his sister, Flo and her family, the professors couldn't do enough for him.

Paul also enjoyed playing the rube. When the MIT engineers took him to see the 60-storey John Hancock skyscraper, he pretended to be unimpressed. His only comment was: "Jaysus, you could put a lot of hay in there."

His hosts took him to an up-market restaurant, Igoe's in Cambridge, for dinner. Paul was in his element.

On the way in, he had a tug of war with the hat check lady.

"A handsome woman tried to take my coat. It was my coat. I paid for it."

They were escorted into a lounge for pre-dinner drinks. Five of them were squeezed around a small round cocktail table.

"Jaysus, are they going to feed the five of us around this small table? I've got bigger milking stools."

There was sawdust on the floor. Patrons were shelling peanuts and discarding the shells on the floor.

"Jaysus, if you threw shells on the floor at Jasper's Restaurant in Sydney, they'd throw you out on your ear."

Paul allowed that the food tasted "wonderful, marvellous, whatever it is; if the restaurant paid their electricity bill maybe we'd be able to see what we are eating."

With a straight face, he kept the other diners in stitches.

On the way out, he had another tussle with the checkroom lady.

"She wanted 50¢. I had to buy it back from her."

PAUL'S stories stood tall. He told one of a retired couple who spent their summers nearby. The wife had her lady friends up for a week every summer and they played bridge non-stop.

Her husband was relegated to the front porch to read the *Cape Breton Post* and the Antigonish *Casket*. The highlight of his week was waving to the Mi'kmaq driving to and from Eskasoni.

Then, his bored, frustrated mind hatched a devilish plan. All week, he saw well-padded, blue-rinse matrons sashay across the lawn en route to the privy. Without being observed, he snaked a garden hose through the grass and into the back of the outhouse. He jammed a funnel into each end of the hose and he waited.

Finally, HMS Marlborough entered harbour.

He waited thirty seconds for her to ensconce herself on the throne. Then, he yelled into the funnel at his end: "Can you hold it a second, lady? We're trying to paint down here."

Paul claimed the poor lady flew out the door like "she was shot from a cannon, her step-ins at half mast."

Paul took me "picking" (antiquing) one cold winter day. We were looking for Nova Scotia pressed glass, embossed stoneware pop bottles, MacAskill photographs and a spinning wheel.

There was no bridge at Grand Narrows in the 1960s. A ferry linked Grand Narrows with Iona. This day, the Barra Strait was jammed with drift ice.

Paul saw the worried look on my face and said: "The ferry is on call. It's over on the other side. There is a telephone in that shack. Crank it and the ferry will come and get us."

I went into the shack. The only appointments were the telephone and a huge photo of the captain and thirty-one crew members of the ferry *Caribou*, who were killed when she was torpedoed off Newfoundland in 1942. At least there wasn't a Muzak recording of "Nearer My God To Thee" or "Autumn."

Paul had only a trace of a grin when this white-faced travelling companion got back in his pick-up truck.

PAUL lived and died by the sword. While Liberals governed Nova Scotia for twenty-three consecutive years, he was assured of steady work. Bob Stanfield's Conservatives ended Liberal rule October 2, 1956. On October 3, Paul was fired.

He was 85 when he died. His battered straw hat hangs from a nail in Donnie and Terry McAdam's cottage. No self-respecting horse would wear a hat like that, but it is the most prized object in the room.

Looking at it, one can almost conjure up a phantasm of Paul saying, with a glint in his eye: "No, I never married. I never had to because I discovered sliced bread and the electric blanket early. I like my 'shine clear and strong, stirred or shaken, and I like telling stories. Yes, I'm a well balanced Scot; I have a chip on both shoulders."

SEA WOLF
ALEX MACLEAN

Prolific American novelist Jack London, author of such classics as *Call of the Wild* and *White Fang*, hoboed around Canada and the United States. He followed the Gold Rush to the Klondike. While in the north, he met up with a colourful sea captain by the name of Alexander MacLean, of East Bay, Cape Breton.

Alex MacLean and his older brother, Dan, were sailing on the Bras d'Or Lakes from the time they could walk. Local Scots joked that the MacLeans had sailed alongside Noah.

When London wrote his novel *Sea Wolf* in 1904, there was little doubt who the hero – a tough, brawling sea captain named Wolf Larsen – was modelled after.

Actually, Jack London's and Captain Alex MacLean's paths had crossed several times – not just in the Klondike. They also met in the saloons of San Francisco, along

Captain Alexander MacLean

Fig. 4. Sketch of Capt. Alex MacLean, "Sea Wolf." Drawn from a photograph taken in Victoria BC, in 1884. Artist unknown.

the Oakland, California, waterfront and probably Pacific Northwest sealing waters.

When the best-selling novel appeared, MacLean jokingly threatened to throw the author into the ocean for portraying him as the Swedish sea captain, Wolf Larsen, rather than a Cape Breton Scot.

The careers of Alex and Dan MacLean and Jack London paralleled each other in other ways. They all left school at early ages to follow the sea. The MacLeans had a strict Scottish religious upbringing from God-fearing parents, but London, said to be the illegitimate son of itinerant astrologer William Henry Chaney, was raised by a family with neither fixed address nor fixed occupation.

London left school at age 14, bought a sloop and raided oyster beds along Oakland Bay. The MacLeans headed for the northern sealing grounds on board the schooner *City of San Diego*, with older brother Dan as skipper and Alex as first mate. The Pacific northwest sealing grounds were considered to be the private hunting preserves of Russia, the United States and Britain. The Alaska Commercial Company owned a 20-year lease on the Aleutian sealing area and their monopoly was reinforced by U.S. revenue cutters. This was a minor inconvenience to the MacLeans, however, and they ignored it completely, poaching at will.

The brothers were probably the most successful seal hunters on the west coast. In 1886, Captain Dan returned to port with a record 4,250 skins and Alex trailed behind him with 3,300. Their combined harvest was a prize valued at more than $60,000. In 1888, Alex dropped anchor in Victoria with what he believed to be the largest cargo of sealskins ever landed.

When he learned that a rival sealer had off-loaded an even larger catch, he put out on a second hunt and returned with the indisputably largest number of sealskins ever landed in Victoria.

Normally, the MacLeans sailed out of Victoria flying the Red Ensign. Once, sailing the *J. Hamilton Lewis*, Captain Dan was challenged by a Russian gunboat which, by sheer coincidence, was named *Alexander*. Captain Dan had no qualms about running up the Stars and Stripes and ignoring the armed Russian patrol boat. The ruse worked.

On another occasion, Captain Alex was caught raiding a seal rookery on Copper Island by the Russians. He was bracketed by Russian gunfire and a crew member drowned when he was swept overboard. The Russian gunship ordered Alex to heave to, but he ignored the warning. More shots were fired and the Russian vessel *Aleut* steamed down across MacLean's bow, carrying away his ship's forerigging.

An armed Russian party boarded MacLean's ship and escorted her to Petropaulovski and then on to Vladivostock where the crew was interned briefly on board their own ship. They were permitted to roam the Russian town freely by day but had to be back on board their ship by 2000 hrs.

Even as a prisoner of the Russians, Alex MacLean's brawling habits came to the fore. As he was crossing over mud on duckboards, he was confronted by three bemedalled Russian officers from the local garrison. They were walking three abreast.

Alex MacLean had no intention of being deferential and yielding to the three Russian militia officers who soon found themselves up to their necks in mud. Soldiers rushed to their aid and Alex was frog-marched back to his lock-up.

A tribunal later found Alex MacLean innocent of poaching or any wrongdoing, but his long incarceration meant that he had missed the season's seal hunt. Not to worry. Off he went to the Yukon to dig for gold. He found accommodation at a hotel in Bennett City owned by a MacNeil, a distant cousin from Washabuck.

Alex wasn't in Bennett City long before he was warned of a card cheat in the hotel's saloon. The crooked gambler played with two loaded pistols on the table in front of him. Alex called him a cheat and was immediately challenged to a duel.

MacLean said that he had the right to choose the distance over which they would fire at one another and the card cheat agreed.

MacLean said: "All right, you stand on one side of the card table and I'll stand on the other side. Now."

The cheat would have no part of MacLean's point blank distance and pleaded for his life.

MacLean disarmed the cheat, administered a severe thrashing and threw him outside into a cold northern snowbank.

Alex's hunting was not restricted to seals or gold. He spent some time in the South Seas poaching French oyster beds for pearls. The French harvested the rich pearl beds every ten years. MacLean plundered them in the ninth year. But he was spotted by a French gunboat.

His ship, *Carmecita*, sailing under Mexican registry, was forced to leave. The crew had hidden their booty in tar pitch between the ship's planks. He told the French he had anchored in the lagoon to take on fresh water and fish. The French found no evidence of pearls on board, but they were suspicious and MacLean's ship was impounded nonetheless.

Under cover of darkness and an approaching storm, the real life Sea Wolf and his crew overpowered their guards, rowed their ship out of the lagoon, set full sail and were never seen again by the French. A Maritime historian, W. A. Claymore, wrote that the French gunship "couldn't have caught them had they tried." Most of the schooners being used by sealers were Maritimers, direct forebears of the fast schooner *Bluenose*.

After the voyage, Captain Alex sported a new tie pin – a pink pearl set in five golden claws.

Alex MacLean was a fierce looking sea captain. His trademark was an 18-inch moustache that he could tie in a knot at the back of his neck. He was five foot eleven and weighed 190 pounds. Reports of his brawling prowess are legendary.

Once, he took exception to negligence of his 230-pound first mate. The mate had allowed several crew members to jump ship and join another sealing vessel (which happened to be his brother Dan's ship). Alex announced he was "going to give him (the first mate) a thrashing."

He ordered the crew below, battened the hatches, took off his shirt and, for half an hour, punched his first officer senseless. MacLean didn't have a scratch on him after the fisticuffs. But he didn't bear a grudge, he considered his mate a good seaman, dressed his cuts and scrapes, shook hands with him and kept him on as second in command.

Like Alex MacLean, Jack London's fictional character Wolf Larsen was the skipper of a sealing ship. They were both known for their great physical power, but Alex MacLean did not possess Larsen's ruthless nature. Back home in East Bay, he was known for his kindness and his generosity with money.

London's idols were Marx and Nietzsche who were poles apart in their ideologies and London championed them – first one and then the other – both in his life and in his novels. Alex MacLean probably never heard of either and historians disagree whether or not he could read.

He probably would not have grasped the symbolism behind London's story, the cult of "red blood" and a breed of Nietzschean supermen engaged in various and violent inner and outer struggles.

CAPTAIN MacLean never left the sea. He was captain of *Favorite* when he accidentally drowned in Vancouver harbour in 1914 at the age of 56. There were reports that, in his lifetime, he had killed 50, men but he maintained he never killed anyone "though I have *lost* 59 men." It has also been recorded that he marooned sailors who fell afoul of his iron discipline.

Once, he told a crew member: "If you want to go ashore, swim for it," and threw him overboard.

Jack London put the sea behind him at a young age and tramped through Canada and the United States for two years before enrolling at the University of California for one semester. He contracted scurvy in the Klondike and returned home to Oakland to write. Until his death in 1916, he wrote 19 novels and scores of short stories.

London's best-selling works made him as popular in the English-speaking world as Rudyard Kipling.

Alex MacLean, the real life Sea Wolf, never did get to carry out his threat to throw Jack London into the Pacific Ocean.

FIRST IN FILM

DANIEL PETRIE

Hollywood film director Dan Petrie was like the Energizer Bunny. He just kept going and going. He was 83 when he passed away in Hollywood on August 22, 2004. When I spoke to him three weeks before his sudden death, he told me he was putting finances together for a movie he wanted to shoot on Sable Island.

Dan blazed the way to Broadway stages and Hollywood for other Canadian directors. His career began in New York in 1950 when Norman Jewison, Arthur Hiller and Fletcher Markle were cutting their teeth with CBC Toronto. Academy Award winning director James Cameron was but a gleam in his parents' eyes.

Along the way, Dan sired a family dynasty that has amassed two Oscar nominations, 11 Emmy Awards, 15 Emmy nominations, 11 Directors' Guild award nominations and dozens of Golden Globe, Screen Writers Guild, Peabody, Christopher and Cannes Film Festival nominations and awards. In 1961, Dan was recognized by the Cannes Film Festival with the award of the Humanitarian Award for *A Raisin in the Sun*.

Some of Dan's credits on TV and screen are: *The Defenders, Medical Centre, The Bold Ones, Studio One, East Side/West Side, Marcus Welby, MD, Kissinger and Nixon, Inherit the Wind, Lassie, The Betsy, Lifeguard, The Return, Cocoon* and *My Favourite Martian*.

Petrie family films have earned their studios half a billion U.S. dollars. None has ever lost money for a studio.

Dan made TV history in 1977 when he directed three of the five Emmy Award nominees. Sally Field was voted Best Actress for her role in *Sybil*. Ed Flanders won Best Actor Award for *Harry Truman – Plain Speaking*. *Eleanor and Franklin* tied for Best Production. For a second consecutive

Fig. 5. *This portrait of Hollywood director Dan Petrie graced the cover of a booklet that was distributed at a Toronto Screen Directors' memorial tribute to Dan. Photographer unknown. Courtesy of Dorothea Petrie.*

year, Dan was named Best Director. He crowned his hat trick by winning a coveted Peabody Award for *Sybil*.

He directed Ellen Burstyn and Eva LeGallienne to Academy Award nominations for *Resurrection*.

His oldest son, Daniel Jr., is past president of the Screen Writers Guild. He was nominated for an Academy Award for his original screenplay of *Beverley Hills Cop*. He wrote *The Big Easy*, featuring Dennis Quaid. He co-wrote and produced *Shoot to Kill* starring Sidney Poitier, Tom Berenger and Kirstie Alley. He co-wrote and produced *Turner and Hooch* starring

Tom Hanks and Hooch, a loveable, but ugly, slobbering dog.

Daniel Jr. also adapted Michael Connelly's *The Concrete Blonde* for Paramount and wrote the screenplay for *Tomorrow Never Dies*, a James Bond flick.

His younger brother Donald directed Disney's *My Favorite Martian*, which starred Jeff Daniels, Christopher Lloyd, Elizabeth Hurley and Daryl Hannah.

Fig. 6. *Dan's wife, Dorothea, was a leading actress on radio "soaps" when they married. She put her career on hold to raise their family of two boys and two girls, but resumed it with a vengeance and amassed an impressive list of major nominations and awards for her film, documentaries and dramas. Photographer unknown. Courtesy Petrie family.*

Donald directed Whoopi Goldberg in *The Associate*, Macaulay Culkin in *Richie Rich* and Jack Lemmon, Walter Matthau and Ann- Margret in *Grumpy Old Men*.

His TV credits include *MacGyver, The Equalizer, L.A. Law* and Steven Spielberg's *Amazing Stories*. Samuel Goldwyn, Jr. handpicked him to direct his first feature film, *Mystic Pizza*, which introduced Julia Roberts to the screen. An episode of *L.A. Law* brought him Emmy and Directors Guild nominations.

The mother of this amazing family, Dorothea ("Dotty"), an actress from Oklahoma, was a star on daytime radio soap shows when she married Dan. She took time off to raise a family and then returned to films with a vengeance.

She has won three Emmys, Directors Guild and Screen Writers Guild Awards, a Christopher, a Peabody and Monte Carlo Film Festival awards. She has directed and produced *Hallmark Hall of Fame*, Proctor and Gamble, General Motors and Dupont TV shows.

DAN SR. was born in the hardscrabble coal mining town of Glace Bay. His father, Will Mark, a soft drink bottler, was wiped out by the Depression. Dan and I joked over the phone about how his father and mother took in boarders to make ends meet.

My own father and mother were two such boarders. When they married in 1929 there were no honeymoon cottages or coal company half-double rental houses for newly-weds. So, they "took rooms at Will Mark Petrie's."

Somehow, the Petrie family scraped money together to send Dan to St. FX University, where he roomed with Danny Gallivan.

Dan Petrie went off to war in 1942 with the First Light Anti-Aircraft Regiment. He was seriously injured in England, underwent surgery on both kidneys and spent seven months in hospital.

After the war, he became the first Canadian soldier to study in the United States under the veterans' resettlement program. He earned a Master's degree

Fig. 7. Dan Petrie (centre) on the set of Fort Apache. The Bronx, with actors Ed Asner (left) and Paul Newman. The photo appeared in the Toronto Screen Directors' tribute booklet. Photographer unknown. Courtesy Petrie family.

from Columbia and a doctorate from Northwestern.

He started his career on a New York stage, a chance meeting with Broadway producer Herman Shumlin landing him a part in *Kiss Them for Me* with Richard Widmark and Judy Holliday. From there, he went on to a major role with a road company of *I Remember Mama*.

When that show folded prematurely, he decided that a career on the other side of the stage lights was more secure. He decided that his first Broadway appearance was "a fluke" because "with my unusually cheerful cherubic looks at five foot eight, nobody was casting Mickey Rooney look-alikes."

Right out of left field, his phone rang and the voice on the other end said: "This is Billy Rose." Dan says he replied: "Yeah, and I'm Louis B. Mayer." It really was Billy Rose and he wanted Dan to direct one of his TV shows.

The offer fell through, though. When Dan read the first script, he decided it was a "bow-wow."

His next career move was a step backward. His first Broadway play was a thinly veiled story of Whittaker Chambers and Alger Hiss, titled *A Shadow of My Enemy*. It closed after only five performances, but Dan caught the eye of New Yorker critic, Wolcott Gibbs.

Next, he was offered the stage adaptation of Budd Shulberg's novel *The Disenchanted*—a saga of F. Scott Fitzgerald.

His first Hollywood film *The Bramble Bush*, with Richard Burton, Barbara Rush, Jack Carson and Angie Dickinson, is less than memorable. Leonard Maltin gives it half a star. However, it led to *A Raisin in the Sun*, which starred Sidney Poitier, Ruby Dee and Louis Gossett Jr., Maltin gave it four stars.

Dan's list of credits is a history of TV and movies. He has directed Helen Hayes, Sir Cedric Hardwicke, Robert Morley, Julie Harris, Richard Burton, Jason Robards,

Fig. 8. Dan Petrie and Danny Gallivan were room mates while attending St. FX University in the late 1930s. Photographer unknown. Courtesy Gary Gallivan, Whitney Pier Museum.

Laurence Harvey, Sir Lawrence Olivier, Burt Lancaster, Tommy Lee Jones, Robert Duvall, Susan Hayward, William Shatner, Winona Ryder, Christopher Plummer, Rob Lowe, Don Harron, Barbara Rush, Sir John Gielgud, John Colicos, Joanne Woodward, Barry Morse, Jane Fonda and Paul Newman.

Jane Fonda's career was in eclipse, until Dan coaxed an Emmy Award winning performance out of her in the TV drama *The Dollmaker.*

Sally Field was Burt Reynold's dippy moll in *Smokey and the Bandit* and a flying nun in a sappy TV series, until Dan showcased her in *Sybil* and she won an Emmy.

Paul Newman's career was stalled, until Dan starred him in *Fort Apache: The Bronx.* Newman's rebirth led to back-to-back Oscar nominations for his next two films: *The Verdict and Absence Of Malice.*

Dan directed the first live TV dramas, and he also directed the last live telecast— *Dupont Show of the Month* with Julie Harris, Jo Van Fleet and E. G. Marshall.

He said he was glad to see the end of live TV drama "because with millions at stake, live TV drama had a great potential for disaster and was extremely nerve-wracking."

Dan said he felt more relaxed directing movies like *Cocoon: The Return*, with Brian Dennehy, Wilford Brimley, Don Ameche,

Hume Cronyn, Jessica Tandy, Gwen Verdon and Maureen Stapleton.

In 1972, Dan directed *The Neptune Factor*, which starred Ben Gazzara and Ernest Borgnine. It was filmed partly in Halifax and gave Nova Scotia's film industry an important leg-up.

ONE OF my most memorable evenings was the night Dan's niece, Mona, invited me to dinner at her flat in Knightsbridge, London. We were almost through the soup course when there was an unexpected knock on the door.

It was Dan. He was in London supervising the musical score for *Rocket Gibraltar* at Pinewood Studios in London and Munich. Eight year-old Macaulay Culkin was putty in Dan's hands and Burt Lancaster was the consummate pro.

For the next three hours we too were putty in Dan's hands. He kept us mesmerized with rib splitting stories of Richard Burton, Jennifer Jones, Elizabeth Taylor, Bob Hope, Rock Hudson, Richard Boone, Raymond Burr, James Woods, James Garner, Pat Boone, Nancy Kwan and scores of other stars he directed.

Dan took pains to set the record straight about Richard Burton's alcohol consumption.

"He never showed up under the weather. He never drank on set or during the lunch break. But, when shooting stopped at 5 p.m. and he snapped his fingers; if his man-servant valued his life, he had to be standing right next to him with a fresh drink in his hand."

The evening was sheer magic.

DAN owned 80 acres of prime land in Baddeck to which he hoped to retire, but he was too much in demand. He donated the land to Cape Breton University.

Dan was diagnosed with cancer and three weeks later – on August 22, 2004 – he died in his sleep at home. The Motion Picture Academy saluted him during the April 2005, televised Academy Awards. The Atlantic Film Festival in Halifax presented a retrospective of Dan's films.

Dan's wife, Dorothea (Dotty), emailed me to advise that Norman Jewison and the Center for Advanced Film Studies had a beautiful Memorial Dinner in Dan's honour. St. Francis Xavier University joined with the Canadian Consulate of Los Angeles to celebrate Dan's life and work.

The Directors Guild of Canada honoured Dan with a posthumous Lifetime Achievement Award in Toronto in October, 2005.

Despite his hectic 24 TV series, Kiefer Sutherland flew in to present the award. Dan gave 15-year old Kiefer his first feature film-starring role in *The Bay Boy* and Kiefer "fondly related how Dan's fatherly advice and support has stayed with him throughout his career."

Sutherland said: "Dan gave me my opportunity. Not only did he do that; he showed me a standard of quality and excellence in production that I still use as a measuring stick today."

AT HIS request, Dan was buried at sea and his Hollywood peers eulogized him at a Los Angeles memorial service.

NOVA SCOTIA'S FIRST DFC

DAVID ROMANS

Residents of the tiny Norwegian fjord village of Bygland (population: 1,500) have not forgotten seven brave RAF pilots who died when their B-17c "Flying Fortress" was shot down by two German Me 109s on September 8, 1941. The bomber crashed in a mountainous area, a half hour trek from the village.

A few days later, the Luftwaffe buried the crew members in a mass grave in the Bygland Protestant Church cemetery. They were later exhumed and re-buried in separate plots and the Commonwealth War Graves Commission erected conventional gravestones.

For sixty years the villagers of Bygland have placed freshly cut flowers on the graves every day. They take turns manicuring the grass around the flyers' last resting places.

Recently the entire village of Bygland forgot the country's national election campaign for a few hours and paid homage to the seven RAF dead buried there.

Floyd Williston, of Sydney and Winnipeg, dedicated a marker and placed a wreath at the crash site in the mountains. Williston is the author of *Through Footless Halls Of Air* – stories of a few of the many who failed to return. His book includes a 56-page account of the final flight of AN525 and her crew.

Two of the Flying Fort's crews were Canadians in the RAF – Flying Officer David Romans of Glace Bay and Halifax, Nova Scotia, and Flight Sergeant Air Gunner, Henri Merrill, of Montreal. F/O Romans was a pilot.

F/O Romans' nephew, John Romans, a retired Halifax lawyer, placed a wreath at the Bygland graveside and spoke at a memorial dinner. Floyd read messages from friends and relatives of F/O Romans and F/S Merrill – including one from F/S

Merrill's brother Jean, of Montreal. The Canadian Embassy in Oslo was represented by the Defence Attaché, Army Colonel Ron Aitken.

The keynote speaker at the dinner was Major Bjorn Robstad of the Norwegian Air Force who gave a riveting account of David Romans' last flight.

ON September 8, 1941, four Flying Fortresses took off from Kinloss, Scotland, at 0915 hours. Their target was the German pocket battleship Admiral Scheer, a sister ship of the Graf Spee. On September 4, the British had learned that the Admiral Scheer had put to sea and was observed entering the Oslo Fjord.

Shortly after take-off, all contact was lost with Fortress AN533 and her crew. They are presumed to have gone down into the sea.

At Sola Air Station, German fighters scrambled. They soon picked up the condensation trails typical of the B-17c. A short, intense air battle followed. F/O Romans jettisoned his bomb load to gain altitude, but the battle was uneven. One Messerschmitt was damaged or destroyed, but AN525 was shot down – the first Flying Fortress downed in World War II. The Luftwaffe was so excited over their kill, they had the wreckage transported to Berlin to examine U.S. bomber technology more closely.

A third Fortress was unable to penetrate a fog bank 140 km from the target and returned to Kinloss after dumping his "cookies" in the sea.

The fourth bomber was badly damaged, but managed to limp back to Kinloss for a wheels-up landing. The plane was written off. The pilot, Flight Sergeant Mick Wood, an Australian, lived to complete 60 sorties over enemy territory and now lives in Tasmania.

Mick Wood saw David Romans's plane going in. There were no parachutes.

David's luck had run out.

Floyd says F/O Romans flew 38 bombing ops over Germany and another 20 "gardening" (mine-laying) and "nickel" missions (leaflet drops) over Germany or German occupied soil.

David's brother Fred told Floyd: "From his letters, I estimate that there were 15 or so occasions when his plane was shot down or barely managed to stagger home."

HE WAS nursing a badly damaged Hampden medium bomber home, but had to ditch a quarter-mile mile off Salthouse Marsh, England. The crew waded ashore only to be waved off by British soldiers. The beach had been mined.

F/O Romans flew a full tour on Hampdens – an unlikely-looking plane that was sometimes mistaken for a German Dornier Do-17 and came under "friendly" fire from RAF fighters. It had a "pod and boom fuselage" and, from the side, looked like a bulbous thermometer.

It was a strange looking design with a short, pencil thin fuselage and a big tail boom that carried twin tail fins. It was nicknamed "flying suitcase" or "flying panhandle" or "flying coffin." The four man crew was wedged in the forward pod and, once in place, it was impossible for the crew to switch places in flight. Pop-gun defensive armament, a small bomb load capacity and short range caused the RAF to abandon it in 1942.

F/O Romans graduated to a "turkey," which was obsolete before it made its first operational flight. The "Manchester" was under-powered by two Rolls Royce 24-cylinder "Vulture" engines. It was re-designed, given four Rolls Royce "Merlin" Mk III engines and became the work horse darling of Bomber Command – the "Lancaster."

Romans was navigator and bomb-aimer on a Hampden on July 18, 1940. The pilot received a shrapnel wound to his head that would prove to be fatal. The bomber plunged into a dive and flew erratically. Romans had to sit on the unconscious pilot's knees to gain control of the plane.

With great difficulty, the pilot was removed from under him 20 minutes later and Romans navigated and flew the plane safely home to base – all the while flying at a dangerously low altitude under intense and accurate anti-aircraft fire.

His homecoming was not without incident. As his wheels touched down, he discovered the brakes were malfunctioning. He swung the plane across the grass, tipping one wing, and broadsided the station adjutant's car, which "shot across the tarmac like a stray bullet."

On July 20, 1940, Air Vice Marshall A. T. ("Bomber") Harris minuted F/O David Romans's recommendation for the Distinguished Flying Cross. His decoration appeared in the London Gazette on July 30. En route to London to receive his "gong" from King George VI at Buckingham Palace, the plane carrying him crashed and had to be written off.

David Romans made it safely to "Buck House" and the king pinned the DFC on him.

He was twenty years old. He was the first Nova Scotian airman to be awarded a Distinguished Flying Cross.

Little more than a year later, the 21 year-old warrior was dead, but the grateful villagers of Bygland will never allow his memory to die.

THE DUKE OF SENATOR'S CORNER

DR. "DUKE" MACISAAC

The professional shingle outside his second floor office in the MacRae block on Senator's Corner was modest – "S. G. MacIsaac, Dentist" – in gold letters on a black background. Oldtimers in Sydney and Big Pond knew Stephen George MacIsaac as "Steve," but to his wife Sally and close friends he was "Duke." Everyone else in Glace Bay called him "Doctor Duke."

For almost half a century, until his death on March 28, 1972, his surgery looked out on rough-and-tumble Senator's Corner and the still rougher saloons of Lower Main Street.

"Duke" MacIsaac was an outstanding amateur, semi-pro and professional goal tender. He played briefly for Sydney Millionaires, then for Glace Bay Miners and a powerful Dalhousie team. He was substitute goalie for the professional Toronto Saint Patrick's, 1922 Stanley Cup champions who later became the Maple Leafs. The St. Patrick's paid him $80 a month and expected him to work a full-time 40-hour week besides, for Imperial Tobacco, one of the team's sponsors.

He had earned more than that from a regular newspaper route and his lucrative newspaper stand outside the main gate of the Sydney Steel Plant.

The "Duke" earned his nickname because, even as a child, he was a dapper dresser.

His first job was as bookkeeper for Harris Abattoir, a predecessor of Canada Packers, in New Waterford, Sydney and New Glasgow. In 1917, he and Alex Kerr, Glace Bay, joined the Royal Flying Corps and earned their pilot's wings at Port Credit, Ontario. They lived in tents during the especially cold winter of 1917-1918. Their friend, Nap Buckley, owned a spare apartment above his chemist's store and he offered "Duke" and Alex free rent if they would work for him part-time.

Their job was bottling, labelling and shipping Buckley's Mixture Cough Syrup on evenings and weekends.

When he was demobbed as a Lieutenant pilot, he came home to Sydney in 1918 and the Millionaires offered him $1 a game. By then he was netting between $100 and $200 a month selling/delivering *Post Record* newspapers and he had "two or three other guys" working for him.

He asked the hockey team for $2 a game, but they refused because he was "local." He went out to Glace Bay to talk to friends Jack Lawlor, Jimmie Fraser and Jack I. MacNeil, and they immediately arranged for him to meet with Mike Dryden, the manager of the Glace Bay Miners. Dryden offered him $5 a game on the spot.

From 1919 to 1923 he played hockey as a sideline, but never again played for his hometown Millionaires. He had also played in New Glasgow. While he was there the *Mont Blanc* and *Imo* collided in Halifax harbour and he said he heard the boom of the Halifax explosion.

His son, Lionel "Web," of Scarborough, Ontario, relates that when he played with the New Glasgow "Black Foxes," opposing rink managers in Pictou and Truro would "darken the lights around the Duke's net and that way they could score. Sometimes on a breakaway or a jam around the net they'd turn off the lights."

Web says that hockey great Bobby Beaton told him "Duke was impregnable"

in nets. There were no blocker or trapper gloves for goalies in the Duke's era. The netminder wore regular hockey gloves with long thin sticks sewn into the leather to protect the backs of the hands. Duke had every one of his fingers broken at least once and "the backs of his hands, those little bones, were all in pieces for the remainder of his life. Did you ever notice Duke's hands were all crooked from his days in hockey? His fingers were crooked from being broken so often."

"Doctor Duke" kept up the friendships he made playing hockey. Every Christmas he touched base by phone with Ottawa Senators owner T. P. Gorman, and Conn Smythe and "King" Clancy of the Toronto Maple Leafs. As well, he maintained his network of hockey friends with pro teams in the U.S.

THE Duke graduated from St. FX High School in 1912, but didn't resume his studies until 1922 when he enrolled at Dalhousie. J. E. "Gee" Ahern, sportswriter, former mayor of Halifax and former president of the Nova Scotia Sport Hall of Fame wrote: "When mythical all-star hockey teams were chosen in the Maritimes in the early twenties, the name of Dr. Stephen "Duke" MacIsaac always appeared as the first choice."

"...he was a brilliant performer not only against the amateurs ... but he also showed his class against the pros in exhibition games. The Dal team in 1920 was one of the best amateur teams in Canada.

"…the great Duke, who could have joined the professionals any day in the week was more interested in winning his degree from the dental school."

Upon graduation, he returned to play hockey in Glace Bay and rented a dental office in the Xidos Block. He lost everything, including his newly financed equipment, in a major fire. A distant relative through marriage, Jack MacRae, came to his rescue. He helped set him up a practice in the MacRae Block, rent free until he could afford it. Jack MacRae pegged Duke's rent at $50 a month – never to be increased – and, when he died, stipulated in his will the dentist's rent would always remain at $50 monthly.

Throughout the years, some of his office neighbours included Mr. Justice J. Louis Dubinsky, E. MacKay Forbes, Lauchie (L. D.) Currie (the man who nominated Angus L. Macdonald for the Liberal leadership and who later served as attorney general), Colonel the Honourable Gordon S. Harrington, Conservative Premier from 1930 to 1933 when he was defeated by Angus L., as well as those giants of Cape Breton's labour movement, District 26, United Mine Workers.

In the late 1930s and early 1940s, Dr. "Duke" was the driving force behind the construction of the Miners' Forum. Web MacIsaac recalls: "Our living room was full of people two or three evenings a week, and Sally was wild. Some of them would arrive at our house with the smell of alcohol, which Sally could notice 100 feet distant."

Minor patronage was not beneath Dr. Duke. One of the workers he hired to do rough carpentry and electrical and plumbing work on the Forum was his friend from Big Pond, Neilie John "The Widow" MacNeil, Rita MacNeil's father. By 1941-1942, his wife Sally had persuaded him to step aside and he turned the Miners' Forum general manager's job over to Martin "The Ape" MacDonald.

The MacIsaacs had a lifelong love affair with Big Pond. Their summer bungalow was perched up on a hill and looked down on St. Andrew's Channel. The bungalow rocked with laughter and Gaelic when the Big Pond parish priest, Father Stanley MacDonald, brother to Angus L., came to play cards. Father Stanley chewed MacDonald's Twist tobacco non-stop. He aimed for the fireplace, but always managed to miss and hit the hearth.

DR. DUKE made a comfortable but modest living in his dental practice. Extractions ranged from $1.50 to $2.50. To supplement his income and support his family of four boys, he took on the job of school dentist. He would set up shop at Central School and children from all the town schools came to him. He was paid $1,500 yearly by the Town of Glace Bay and

20 years later his annual stipend was still $1,500.

He saw thousands of school kids and they eventually wore his nerves down to the point where he was ingesting Pepto Bismal antacid morning, noon and night.

Many of his dental patients couldn't or wouldn't pay, but he never pursued bad debts.

Louis Gefter lived in a small bachelor apartment near Dr. Duke's office. Between the two of them they knew everybody in town and everything that was going on in it. But they weren't gossips. They only told one another.

ONE Christmas Day, Dr. Duke was in the bosom of his family and the delicious smell of a roasting turkey filled the house. The phone rang. It was Louis. He was in terrible pain and wanted Duke to open his office and pull a tooth. Duke walked the mile down Chapel Hill to his office where Louis was waiting almost in tears.

The dentist saw immediately the tooth was infected and he told Louis he wasn't sure he would be able to freeze it. He gave him one injection, which failed to freeze the gums. He tried a second needle, but still there was no relief.

Duke somehow managed to find a taxi driver on duty on Christmas Day and asked him to drop off a bottle of bootleg rum. He poured the rum into Louis until he was in

such state he didn't care if Duke pried the tooth out with a tire iron.

Out it came. Ahhhhhhhh! Relief! Louis was ecstatic.

"How much do I owe you, "Duke"?

One thing Duke was never comfortable around was money, and he hemmed and hawed all the while mentally calculating how much the pain killer, needles, other dental supplies, bootleg rum and a generous tip for the taxi driver had set him back – not to mention his professional services and the fact it was Christmas Day.

"I don't know, Louis, pay me what you think it is worth."

Louis took out his wallet and passed Dr. Duke a $2 bill and wished him a very Merry Christmas.

SALLY MacIsaac died at the wheel of her car when she suffered a heart attack December 8, 1971. Dr. Duke died less than four months later. The MacIsaacs had four sons: Stephen Gregory (Greg) is a retired urologist who now lives in Florida, Lionel "Web," a Human Relations and Labour Relations specialist, passed away in 2002. Donald is a retired accountant and former Cape Breton County Councillor living in Westmount and John Lorne, a teacher, lives in London, Ontario.

DUKE was one of the very first athletes to the named to the hockey section of the Nova Scotia Sports Hall of Fame.

A MOST GENEROUS MAN
JACK MACRAE

Dr. Duke MacIsaac and his family lived comfortably at 143 Main Street across from Afton Hall, the residence of Jack and Jessie MacRae. Afton Hall was by far the largest single-family dwelling in Glace Bay and is now the site of Curry's Funeral Home.

Afton Hall didn't need night watchmen. Jack MacRae's doberman "Bimbo" attacked anything and anyone daring to place even one shoe on the huge property.

Once, Jessie MacRae decided to throw an elaborate banquet for the pilots who had participated in a big air show at the old Cape Breton Flying Field. All the local swells and VIPs were there. Solly Goldman of Glace Bay says the banquet "was a great success and everyone enjoyed themselves. The unfortunate part was that when the guests left, so did the silverware."

JACK MacRae was probably the wealthiest man in Glace Bay. His saloon on Lower Main Street boasted it had the longest bar in the world. There were no stools, just a brass footrail, brass spittoons and sawdust on the floor. The bar had large mirrors and provocative paintings of women on the walls behind it.

There was no cash register in Jack's. In its place was an apple or pork barrel under the bar. Single drinks sold for 25¢ and doubles for 50¢. Bartenders slid coins across the bar and into the barrel. Doctor Duke once said that thirsty patrons lined every inch of the bar, day and night, four to five men deep.

Jack MacRae liked to go up to Senator's Corner every evening with his pockets full of 25¢ and 50¢ pieces. He'd warn the boys hawking newspapers on the corner: "I'm going to throw up, boys" and the sidewalks would be paved with silver.

He was probably the most generous man in Glace Bay. When a small businessman was down on his luck, Jack gave him two puncheons of rum, saying: "Here, sell this and keep the money." The man did and Jack's gift was the grubstake that revived his flagging business venture.

Jack brought in barrels of oysters from Orangedale and sold them on the half-shell at his saloon. He sold rounds of bulk tobacco. There was a cutting device for apportioning the tobacco. It was this cutting device that killed his father when Jack threw it at him in an outburst of temper.

He was tried for his father's death, but the ablest defence lawyer of the day, Jim Madden, obtained an acquittal. Jack and Jessie MacRae named their only son Madden. Years later watched helplessly when he drowned while swimming in the Mira River.

Jack also owned an English bulldog named Hoagie. One day, a drunk kicked Hoagie in the mouth and knocked out most of his teeth.

Jack came to Dr. Duke for cosmetic help for Hoagie. Duke did the impressions and denturist Clarence Andrews fashioned the plate. The dog's new teeth were solid gold.

Glace Bay was one of the main spokes in the hub of smuggled liquor that fast clipper ships brought in from St. Pierre and Miquelon and the Caribbean. The Volstead Act had been passed in the United States. Prohibition was law, but there was still a great national thirst for booze.

When the casks of contraband were landed at Glace Bay, they were buried on Minto Street until it was deemed safe to bottle the smuggled spirits and move them by trucks to the U.S.

One piece of local folklore is that the manager of the local power utility was in the pay of the rumrunners and, on demand, every light bulb in town would be doused so trucks could be loaded and make their fast dash for the Canso ferry. The revenuers were in the dark more ways than one.

Another bit of unsubstantiated lore is that in 1931, two Glace Bay bootleggers drove their fast roadster to Halifax to meet with Chicago mob chief Al Capone who awaited them on board his yacht. Capone was in Halifax to shore up his lines of supply and delivery dates to New York, Boston and Chicago.

One of Jack's best friends was Louis Gefter who handled all of MacRae's finances and rents. He handled all of Mrs. MacRae's affairs and was the chief administrator of their wills. Jack MacRae didn't bank his profits. Louis Gefter stashed the cash away somewhere – perhaps in his apartment.

A. B.

JUDGE A. B. MACGILLIVRAY

Judge Alexander Bernard MacGillivray was one of the most colourful folk characters Cape Breton ever produced. Locals knew him simply as "A. B." His formal education was limited to the village school in his birthplace of Grand Narrows.

Grand Narrows was separated from Iona by a short ferry ride across the Barra Strait in the Bras d'Or Lakes. Iona is the hamlet where the first Scots settled more than two centuries ago. They were Canada's first boat people – poor economic migrants looking for a better life.

A. B.'s family farmed and fished a subsistence living there until he was thirteen. Then they moved to Glace Bay to "dig the coal" alongside other immigrants from Poland, the Ukraine and the Baltic states. A. B. worked at a variety of blue- and white-collar jobs in the coal industry.

When Glace Bay was incorporated as a town in 1901, A. B., then 43, was named the town's first Stipendiary Magistrate and dispensed "common sense justice" for more than 40 years.

A. B. did not attend law school; he had no formal legal training. Late Nova Scotia Justice Leo McIntyre said: "He possessed a knowledge of law far beyond the ken of many learned counsel who pleaded cases in his court."

Judge A. B.'s courtroom sessions were usually SRO – Standing Room Only. Off-duty crown attorneys, defence lawyers, journalists and the curious, looking to be entertained, crowded into his modest court. His court was well worth attending. The air crackled with anticipation of the delights that might follow.

He was earthy, outrageous, witty and pithy, but he displayed the wisdom of Solomon ensuring that justice was done and seen to be done. His judgements positively sparkled. "A. B. stories" are firmly imbedded in Cape Breton folklore.

One morning A. B. found a smug local individual guilty of a misdemeanour and fined him $10 and costs. The accused snickered and said to his lawyer in a loud stage whisper: "That's easy! I got that in me arse pocket."

There wasn't enough time for his stage whisper's echo to die before A. B. chimed in "...and 30 days in the county jail! Have you got that in your arse pocket too?"

A ne'er-do-well transient hobo nicknamed "Boxcar Bill" appeared before A. B. charged with vagrancy. A. B. found him guilty and said, when passing sentence, "Boxcar Bill, I am side-tracking you for 30 days."

In the 1930s, what had to be one of the world's first flower children, a transient, appeared before A. B. It was apparent to A. B. she had found some magic mushrooms somewhere in the highlands of Cape Breton. He asked her what she was doing in Glace Bay and how she got there.

She smiled her best Mary Poppins smile and told him she slid down from heaven on a moonbeam. A. B. asked her if thirty days would be long enough "to get the splinters out of your arse."

A. B.'s most celebrated case involved John and Susie, high school sweethearts. Susie announced she was pregnant. The fathers of the young lovers consulted A. B., who ruled that since there was mutual consent, there was no suggestion of rape.

Neither Susie and John nor their families felt the two minors were ready for marriage. The matter was considered closed when John's father agreed to pay a modest sum for Susie's expenses.

When nine months had elapsed, it became apparent it was a false alarm. Susie was not pregnant. John's father wanted his money back, so the matter landed back in A. B.'s court. He heard the evidence and took the matter under advisement.

After a few days deliberation and much soul searching, A. B. summoned the principals to his courtroom and rendered his judgment. John's father was either to get his money back or John was to "have another crack at Susie."

On another occasion, a wife was in A. B.'s courtroom testifying in a civil action against the Sydney and Louisburg Railway. Her husband had been clipped by the cow-catcher and thrown into alder trees. He was not killed, but he was badly bruised.

A. B. asked the witness to tell the court what happened in her own words.

"What happened? Me and my husband were picking blueberries and the train hit me husband in the arse."

A. B. interrupted her and said: "You must mean rectum?"

"Wrecked him? It damned near killed him!"

A. B. was a big man – six foot two – always turned out in a steel grey suit and derby. He wore wing collars. A heavy watch chain was usually draped over his ample midriff. He wore a carefully trimmed goatee.

He was fastidious in his personal appearance and chose his wardrobe carefully. Once, he went to a gents' furnishing store to buy a size 16 shirt. The clerk selected a box with size 16 stencilled on it, removed a shirt, wrapped it, and A. B. proceeded home. When he tried the shirt on he found it was only a size 12.

He took the shirt back the next morning. The clerk scratched his chin in puzzlement and said it was strange, because the size had been marked on the box from which he had removed the shirt.

A. B. thundered crisply: "It's the goddamned shirt I wear – not the box."

A. B. grew with Glace Bay. When World War II broke out, Glace Bay, with a population of more than 30,000, was Canada's largest town. The coalmines employed 12,000; the Sydney steel plant employed another 7,000 in blast furnaces, coke ovens and rail, wire and nail mills.

Glace Bay's fine natural harbour supported a vibrant fishery – lobsters, cod, halibut, grey ocean perch, flounder, haddock and the undisputed king: swordfish. Some days, as many as 1,000 dressed swordfish, averaging 200-250 pounds each, would be packed in ice-filled coffins and shipped by trucks to buyers in Boston.

When the wind blew northeast, people in Glace Bay could smell the gases from the coke ovens nine miles away. It smelled as sweet as Chanel No. 5 – a guarantee of a fat pay envelope on Friday evening. Unemployment was an unknown and alien word.

GLACE Bay had its own 20-25 man police force, but the Royal Canadian Mounted Police posted its own elite three-man force. The RCMP's only assignment was finding and busting up illicit stills. Moonshine was the "poison" of many discriminating local tipplers – including A. B.

One day, the three Mounties lay in wait in the woods near a still. They saw a man approaching with a 100-pound sack of brown sugar on his back. The still was destroyed and the man was charged with distilling illicit alcohol.

He appeared before A. B. acting as his own lawyer. His first question to A. B. was: "What's illegal about making a little fudge?" A. B. dismissed the charges. The RCMP officers were not amused but, as the locals say: They were from away – they weren't Cape Bretoners.

A. B. kept a milk cow. One day it went missing. He was searching a wooded area near the parish rectory. The pastor suggested A. B. visit the church and "offer up a prayer to St. Anthony, the patron saint of lost items."

A. B. saw little sense in that suggestion and told the priest: "Father, I think I know these woods far better than St. Anthony does."

On one occasion, A. B. left his home for a "short visit" with "a sick friend." He returned home three days later to a frosty reception from his wife Mary. She noticed his clothes were soiled by ash from his pipe. A. B. explained it away by telling her it happened on a streetcar when an inebriated passenger kept brushing up against him and dropping ashes from his pipe.

He told her he would get even in court the next morning, because the drunk was arrested when he stepped down from the streetcar on Senator's Corner. A. B. assured Mary he would make sure the court costs he planned to assess covered his dry-cleaning bill.

The next morning, Mary called A. B. and told him to fine the drunk an extra $20.

"Why?" asked A. B.

"Because, when he put his pipe in your pocket, he burned a hole in the arse of the pants of your best suit."

A. B. wasn't always the star in his own courtroom. One morning, a local madame was testifying and the crown attorney stepped over the line while questioning her. Everyone in the courtroom – including A. B. – knew who she was and what her business was.

But the crown insisted on plodding on. He asked her name, the nature of her business and the location of her brothel.

When the line of questioning had gone on too long – under A. B.'s watchful and mischievous eyes – the madame had enough and stopped the crown attorney in his tracks with an elephant gun reply: "Why are you asking me all these foolish questions? You know all the answers – you've been there often enough yourself."

CAPE Breton's longest running comedy show came to an end in the early 1940s when A. B. retired. He died a few years later.

LAST OF THE BOULEVARDIERS

LARRY SHANAHAN

Every small town has its fools and, on the other end of the spectrum, its *boulevardiers*.

My hometown was no exception.

Newfoundlanders called fools "queer sticks," but said they were "touched by the Hand of God."

Fools could be found at funerals and parades and their only crime was sometimes throwing the drum major out of step. They were accepted for what they were and treated with kindness and great sensitivity.

The boulevardiers were another kettle of fish. They dressed like tweedy British toffs complete with Tattersall shirts, wore freshly cut flowers in their lapels and usually carried a highly polished, gold topped, mahogany Malacca cane.

We had several boulevardiers who stood out like sore thumbs in a working class coal mining town.

Vincent MacDonald was a dapper insurance agent. Hardly anyone remembers him by his Christian name. He was known to everyone as "City Mouse."

If you looked at him and then closed your eyes you could conjure up a mental picture of one of Beatrix Potter's cute comic mice. City Mouse would not be out of place if he had suddenly been beamed off to one of England's shires.

He was so tiny perfect that one local wag said he must have bought himself at Harrod's.

City Mouse died in 1966 and his funeral was one of the largest ever in town.

Larry Shanahan was the last of the grand boulevardiers west of Paris's Left Bank. Larry didn't walk down Main Street in Glace Bay. He strutted. He towered over Main Street like a modern day colossus.

It took forever for him to walk down Main Street to the Town Hall on MacKeen

Street, because so many people stopped to chat him up.

He smoked expensive cigars and cracked off-colour jokes to nuns, priests, spinsters and widows alike. They loved him.

Without a doubt, he was one of the best-dressed men in town, always impeccable in a double breasted Glen Check suit, brilliantly starched white shirt, hand-tied bowtie, waxed moustache and never a strand out of place on his full head of wavy hair.

LARRY was always ready with a joke. He gave every woman he met downtown a kiss – even the good Sisters of Charity from St. Anne's. Only Larry could escape a slap in the face when he told them one of his risqué jokes.

One never knew if Larry's tales were tall or true. One of his stock-in-trade yarns was about the time he took in the 1930s Chicago Exposition. When he returned home, he told everyone in town that Carnation had introduced a new product to the world – canned cream – and held a contest to mark its launch.

Larry said he entered Carnation's jingle contest and won the $1,000 first prize for the best slogan. His winning entry:

> No tits to pull
> No shit to clean
> Just punch two holes
> And out comes cream

ROBERT S. (Bob) MacLellan, the former Tory Member of Parliament for Inverness-Richmond, tells the delightful story of Larry's boyhood in the Low Point area, across the water from North Sydney.

Larry said his father was a "dour, stern old bugger" who presided over the breakfast oatmeal porridge and forbade the children to speak.

After breakfast, Larry picked up his books, held together by a leather strap, and walked to school. One morning, a clipper ship put a longboat over the side at the "Polar Bear" beach at South Bar. They were coming ashore for fresh water.

Larry approached the boat's officer and asked him if they needed a cabin boy. He was told he was in luck and to get aboard. Larry threw his schoolbooks in a cave and went off to sea.

"For seven years I sailed the seven seas, but I missed my family and I thought it was time to go home," Larry said, according to Bob MacLellan. "The next time we anchored off South Bar I asked the captain to put me ashore.

"Just for devilment, I decided to look in the cave where I had throwed me books. Sure, enough they were still there, all green with mould. So, I slung them over my shoulder and skipped along the path to home.

"I went in the back door which opened onto the kitchen. There was me old father, ruling over the breakfast table and doling out ladles of hot oatmeal porridge. He didn't even look up when I came in the door.

"All he said was: 'Larry, were you kept after school'?"

LARRY had no formal training in engineering subjects, but he was the town surveyor in Glace Bay. Locals joke that "the lawyers gave Larry his surveyor's papers and then made a fortune on his measurements."

His "more or less" measurements resulted in many court cases and many neighbours fell out because of an error of "a foot or two."

Glace Bay resident Raymond Goldman remembers when he was a small kid, holding the end of a measuring tape for Larry. "He took such crude measures. Even at my young age I knew he was wrong."

Larry's exuberant personality over-rode his shortcomings. Everyone loved to see him coming. He could light up even a rainy day.

He passed away December 7, 1957, at age 82.

BABE RUTH'S GLACE BAY CONNECTION
BROTHER MATHIAS

At the age of seven, George Herman "Babe" Ruth was pronounced incorrigible.

He was born in Baltimore in 1895, one of eight children born of George Herman and Kate Ruth. Six died in infancy. Only first-born George Herman and sister, Mamie, survived.

Contrary to folklore, he was not an orphan. His father was a bartender who eventually owned his own tavern. The Ruths worked long hours. Young George was left to fend for himself on the tough, hardscrabble Baltimore waterfront. His parents had no time for him. His first seven years were devoid of normal family life or affection.

When his parents decided they could no longer cope with a dead-end kid already engaged in petty thefts and mischief, they took him to St. Mary's Industrial School for Boys and signed over guardianship to the Jesuits' Xaverian Brothers.

St. Mary's was a combination reform school and orphanage, housing 800 children behind prison-like walls. In the dozen years Ruth was there, he did not have a single visitor.

He met disciplinarian Brother Mathias at St. Mary's.

BROTHER Mathias was six-foot-four, 220-pound Cape Bretoner, born Martin Boutilier, July, 1872, in Bridgeport, a Glace Bay suburb. His father was a miner who moved the family to Boston when work petered out in Lingan colliery.

As a kid, Martin played baseball, but is not remembered for his prowess on the diamond. He took Ruth under his wing and coached him in every aspect of the game – pitching, fielding, batting and bunting. He made his protégé master every position.

In an interview with Bob Considine, Ruth recalled Brother Mathias could hold a bat with one hand and lash out 350-foot fly balls. When Ruth was 12, he was playing with 16 year-olds and when he was 16 he was the best all-round player at St. Mary's.

Ruth developed into a hot professional prospect. He was 19, but still legally a minor supposed to remain at St. Mary's until he was 21.

Jack Dunn, manager of the Baltimore Orioles, then a minor league club, skirted the technicality by becoming Ruth's guardian. Dunn was respected as a shrewd judge of talent on the prowl for young potential. When he showed up in the clubhouse with his latest find, veteran players cracked: "Here's Jack with his newest babe."

The nickname stuck and George Herman Ruth was forever known as Babe.

Five months later, July 1914, the Baltimore Orioles sold Ruth to the Boston Red Sox. Boston dealt him to the Yankees in 1919. He powered them to seven pennants and four World Series victories.

BROTHER Mathias may have shaped Ruth into a superb athlete, but his exposure to social graces was minimal. When Ruth played in New York, the wives of Yankees owners Del Webb and Dan Topping asked their husbands to make "Babe" available for a fashionable fundraising luncheon.

Webb and Topping hesitated, because they were well aware of Ruth's sometimes uncouth behaviour. However, they relented and Babe sat at the head table resplendent in a well-tailored double-breasted suit, immaculate white shirt and conservative tie. His hair was perfectly groomed. His rosy, altar-boy cheeks glowed.

The kid from the wrong side of the tracks was Mr. Smooth. He charmed the knickers off the cream of New York society with his impeccable manners. Until one of the ladies passed him a salver: "Asparagus, Mr. Ruth?"

Babe declined. He told the society matron: "Thank you, no. I never eat asparagus. It makes my piss stink."

Brother Mathias did manage to kindle the love Ruth did not enjoy as a child. "Babe" loved kids. Everywhere he went he was a Pied Piper. Children mobbed him and he never discouraged them. He seldom turned down a request to help kids or visit them in hospitals and orphanages. He returned to St. Mary's time and again.

The "Babe" kept in touch with Brother Mathias. So did the Yankees. When Yankees' manager Miller Huggins had trouble handling his free spirit, he phoned Brother Mathias. Ruth gave Brother Mathias a new Cadillac and that must have presented a problem. Brother Mathias had taken a vow of poverty.

BABE Ruth visited Nova Scotia often to hunt and fish, but he never crossed the Strait of Canso to visit Brother Mathias's birthplace. Babe had a hunting buddy in Lockeport. He gave hitting exhibitions in Halifax and Westville in 1936 and 1942. But by then, the "Babe" was in his forties and well past his sell-by date.

He disappointed Halifax fans at Wanderers' Grounds in 1942. The *Halifax Chronicle-Herald* reported that a "rotund Bambino" dressed in street clothes and two-tone brown and white wing-tip shoes waddled to the plate. Local relief pitcher "Aukie" Titus grooved a few fastballs. The Babe swung and missed the first two pitches and then managed a puny fly ball to short right field.

He drove a few line drives down the first base line, popped up to the catcher, fanned on the next three pitches and quit. Enthusiastic Halifax fans expected to see baseballs sprayed over the fence and into the Public Gardens. Before he departed, he picked up a fungo bat and knocked a dozen autographed balls to shallow outfield.

Six years later, August 16, 1948, the Babe went out swinging to cancer. His casket lay in state for two days at the main entrance to Yankee Stadium. Brother Mathias had passed away four years earlier – October 16, 1944 – but Babe Ruth was too ill to attend his funeral in Peabody, Massachusetts.

CHERISHED BY THOUSANDS, VIRTUALLY UNKNOWN

DR. WALTER MACKENZIE

One of the greats of world medicine, Walter Campbell MacKenzie, came from Glace Bay, but he is largely unknown to the average Canadian. The University of Alberta's website makes no personal mention of one of its most famous alumni, other than references to a campus building named after him.

The City of Edmonton's archives provided a sheaf of newspaper articles on his distinguished career in medicine and administration.

His peers awarded him the highest honour the Canadian Medical Association can bestow – the F. N. G. Starr Award, described as the "Victoria Cross of Canadian Medicine," was named for Dr. Frederic Newton Gisborne Starr, Secretary General of the Canadian Medical Association in 1927. Previous recipients were Sir Frederick Banting and Dr.

Charles Best, co-discoverers of insulin, and Montreal neurologist Dr. Wilder Penfield.

In October, 1966, in San Francisco, 12,000 delegates to a convention of the American College of Surgeons acclaimed MacKenzie as their president. The American College has members in 100 countries.

DR. MacKenzie was born in Glace Bay, August 17, 1909. He earned his medical degree from Dalhousie University in 1933, followed by a Master's degree from the University of Minnesota. From 1934 to 1937, he was a Fellow of Surgery at the Mayo Foundation and Mayo Clinic, in Rochester, Minnesota.

In 1938, he established a private practice in Edmonton, Alberta.

He spent six years as a Surgeon Commander in the Royal Canadian Navy during World War II. He served aboard a destroyer on the perilous North Russian run. He said of his naval experience: "I wouldn't trade a day of it."

From 1959 until his retirement in 1974, he served as Dean of Medicine at the University of Alberta. In 1964, he was elected president of the Royal College of Physicians and Surgeons of Canada.

At his retirement dinner, his successor, Dr. D. F. Cameron, said: "From Peking to Moscow to the Arctic to the jungles of Africa, mention Edmonton and they will say 'I have a good friend there in Walter MacKenzie'."

He was the author of 67 papers on surgery and medical education. He was a member of 25 medical societies and he served as president of half of them.

In 1965, he was awarded an honorary fellowship by the Royal College of Surgeons in Edinburgh, Scotland. McGill University conferred an Honorary Doctor of Laws on Dr. MacKenzie. In 1966, his alma mater, Dalhousie, also conferred an Honorary Doctor of Laws.

In 1971, he was the recipient of a Nuffield travelling fellowship to work in Britain and Australia to study and promote community-oriented health services. The wealthy British Lord Nuffield funded the awards.

THE following year, the University of Minnesota presented him with their Outstanding Achievement Award.

Dr. MacKenzie lectured around the world – Nigeria, West Indies, Great Britain and Australia – and in 1962 he was named Sir Arthur Sims' Commonwealth Travelling Professor.

Honours fell on his shoulders like leaves falling from trees. He was Honorary Surgeon to Her Majesty, Queen Elizabeth II, an advisor to the federal Department of Veterans' Affairs, Honorary Fellow of the Royal College of Surgeons of England, Edinburgh, Ireland and Glasgow, and an Honorary Member or Fellow of medical colleges in countries around the world. He was also president of the alumni association of the Mayo Clinic in 1953.

He was awarded the Centennial Medal in 1967 and inducted into the Order of Canada in 1971. The Edmonton chapter of B'nai Brith presented him with their humanitarian service award.

Retirement did not slow him down. In 1976, University of Alberta alumni presented him with their highest accolade – the Golden Jubilee Award. The Province of Alberta appointed him chairman of a provincial task force to investigate highway deaths and suicides. He also served as chairman of an Alberta Cancer Hospital Board.

Dr. MacKenzie was among the first to support the mandatory use of seatbelts in cars. He fretted that young people were "throwing their health away" through alcohol and drug abuse, smoking and poor diets.

He agonized over doctor-patient relationships. He advocated change with the times. He said: "Doctors themselves should be taking a more positive, holistic approach. We should look at why patients are turning away from our services and be prepared to alter our attitudes."

The University of Alberta named their $140 million health sciences building The Dr. Walter Campbell MacKenzie Building.

DR. MacKenzie had two sons and one daughter. Rick is a librarian in Kelowna, BC. Sally studied nursing in Red Deer, Alberta, and Kenneth (Kim) was Alberta's 1966 Rhodes Scholar. Upon graduating from the University of Alberta, Kenneth pursued graduate studies in urban and regional planning at the University of Toronto. He continued his studies in urban geography at Oxford.

The renowned former dean with a global reputation as a surgeon, educator, researcher and administrator died in Edmonton on December 15, 1978, at age 69.

FORMER University of Alberta President Dr. Max Wyman recalled: "He has a truly international reputation and brought great fame to the University of Alberta. He also built one of the finest medical schools in the world."

His epitaph: "Walter MacKenzie was an intellect revered by his students and colleagues and a personality cherished by thousands."

SOLDIERS, PROSPECTORS, FIGHTERS
JACK MUNROE AND BOBBIE BURNS

Jack Munroe was one of the most extraordinary and least known Canadians who ever lived.

John Alexander (Jack) Munroe was born on a farm at Upper Kempt Head, 11 miles from Boularderie, in 1873.

He was a prospector, a hard running star halfback on a championship football team in the highly competitive Western United States high school conference, a five-year professional star in football-mad Montana, a professional boxer and wrestler, a World War I hero, a poet, a gifted author and the reeve of boomtown Elk Lake in northern Ontario. He defeated the heavyweight champion of the world in a four-round bout in Butte, Montana in 1902.

In Ontario's north, he is still remembered as the man who organized the fire brigade that saved Elk Lake in the great Porcupine forest fire of 1911.

He may have been the very first Canadian soldier to set foot on French soil in World War I. Before the ship's gangplank could be fully deployed, Jack jumped from the deck onto French soil.

WHEN he was twelve years old, Jack Munroe and two of his brothers left Cape Breton to seek their fortunes in Nevada and Montana.

Butte was one of the toughest and most lawless mining towns in North America. Standard dress accessories were a pair of Colt revolvers and a Bowie knife. Even feared peace keepers Bat Masterson and Wyatt Earp gave Butte a miss.

On December 20, 1902, Jack defeated world heavyweight boxing champion James J. Jeffries in a four round-bout in Butte. Munroe gave as good as he took for three rounds and then decked the champion for a count of nine in the fourth round. His purse was $250.

In February, 1904 he gave top ranked heavyweight contender Tom Sharkey a fierce beating in a six-round bout in Philadelphia. Sharkey was still on his feet at the end of the fight, but both his eyes were closed. Jack didn't have a mark on him.

Jeffries avenged his humiliating loss to the unknown in August, 1904 when he successfully defended his heavyweight title by knocking out Jack in the second round.

In November, 1904 Jack knocked out Peter Maher, heavyweight champion of Ireland, in the fourth round in Philadelphia.

Jack Munroe had 20 major fights. He lost only three fights and won nine by knockouts.

His last fight was in April, 1906 in Lavigne's Hall in Hull. He knocked out Ottawa's Alf Allen in the eighth round. MUNROE squirreled his wages and fight purses away to invest in prospecting for base and precious metals.

In Mexico City, a fully-grown stray male collie dog adopted him. They bonded immediately and Jack Munroe and "Bobbie Burns" became inseparable. Jack told his friends that in another incarnation Bobbie Burns was Highland royalty.

Bobbie was with Jack when he presented himself at Lansdowne Park, Ottawa, to enlist in the newly formed Princess Patricia's Canadian Light Infantry. The unit was named after Princess Patricia, daughter of Canada's Governor General, the Duke of Connaught, Queen Victoria's youngest son.

The Pats were formed in August, 1914 after wealthy Montreal businessman Hamilton Gault pledged $100,000 for a volunteer infantry battalion. The regiment had the best of equipment – Lee Enfield rifles instead of the unreliable Ross rifles and Penetanguishene boots instead of the shoddy footwear issued to other Canadian troops.

Bobbie Burns enlisted, too. Princess Patricia proclaimed him regimental mascot of the PPCLI. She presented him with an expensive jewelled collar inscribed: Bobbie Burns. PPCLI.

While the regiment was bivouacked at Lévis, Quebec awaiting passage to England, "Bobbie" was kidnapped. Frantic Pats fanned out and searched the countryside. He was found a week later, tied up, at Valcartier. He had refused all food and drink during his captivity.

Bobbie went everywhere with Jack. He was smuggled on board trains, carried onto a troop ship in a gunny sack, slipped past England's animal quarantine inspectors and he followed Jack to the Western Front in the Second Battle for Ypres.

Bobbie Burns was treated as a minor god, from the Colonel on down.

When the PPCLI crossed the English Channel to France, they were 1,000 strong. The regiment was reinforced with drafts of 800 men. When the battle for Ypres was over, there were only 133 left.

Munroe's regiment fought off the Germans under the most appalling conditions: trench warfare, mud, rats, lice, the stench of decaying human and animal flesh, constant artillery barrages, German snipers with newfangled telescope sights that enabled them to pick off a man 2,000 yards away, a shortage of food and ammunition, and two and three days on end without sleep.

Jack told his mining buddies that Bobbie Burns went out with him on "recce" missions. He said that even though Bobbie was a collie, he had all the instincts of a pointer. When he spotted an enemy soldier across no man's land, his body would go rigid and his tail stood straight out.

The Pats stopped the German advance at a heroic, but costly, stand at Pollegon Wood and carried the day. If the Germans had broken through, they would have taken Ypres and bulled their way through to Calais.

Jack led a platoon that captured 90 German prisoners. He wasn't awarded any major gongs for bravery in the living hell that was Ypres. Yet, he earned the highest award possible: he survived.

On June 16, 1916, Jack was shot in the right breast by a sniper near Armentieres. The bullet exited very close to his spinal column. Arterial blood spurted out until one of Jack's comrades stuck his finger in the bullet hole and staunched the flow.

The medical officer told Jack his life depended on remaining perfectly still, lest he bleed to death. Four days later he was invalided to Royal Victoria Hospital in Netley, 70 miles from London. The hospital commandant issued an order that Bobbie Burns would be permitted to stay at Jack's bedside and would have the run of the hospital.

Queen Mother Alexandra, the widow of King Edward VII, visited the wounded soldiers in hospital. Jack noted later in his mini-classic book *Mopping Up* that the Queen Mother met Bobbie and had some "kind words" for him.

"Bobbie was pleased," Jack noted. Bobbie liked attention, but he was not overwhelmed.

Mopping Up was the book Jack wrote in 1918. It was a stark, sensitive and extremely well written first person story told through Bobbie's eyes.

Jack related the incident of the time he was prospecting unsuccessfully in a remote region near Hurst. He caught a train "at a lonely station" and took it for granted that Bobbie was under his seat.

But, the collie had missed the train. Jack believed he "had seen the last of Bobbie."

The train carried Jack to Porcupine. Ten days later, Bobbie arrived there too. He had covered 200 miles of "as rough, unbroken country as there is in the world."

Bobbie was "somewhat thin and not a little weary," but he "upreared and flung his forepaws upon my shoulders, the happiest, wriggling, home-coming prodigal son of a collie in Canada, or in all the world."

Some historians believe that Bobbie and *Mopping Up* were the inspiration for Eric Mowbray Knight when he wrote the classic *Lassie Come Home*.

JACK and Bobbie came home to Canada to dull desk jobs in recruiting offices. Jack was commissioned a lieutenant and given permission to join the Liberty Bond speaking tour in the United States, where he was a popular drawing card. He was discharged in December, 1918.

The pair went to Nova Scotia to visit his ailing mother and family. Their next stop was northern Ontario to claim his fortune in gold and silver mines.

Jack became extremely rich selling claims. But he hadn't fallen off a turnip truck from Boularderie. He kept a small percentage interest in each claim. He parlayed his riches into hotels and commercial office realty in Ontario's northland.

Despite further surgeries, Jack's strong right arm would hang useless at his side for the rest of his life.

BOBBIE Burns was sixteen when he died in 1919. One day he failed to meet Jack's train at the station. He had crawled off into the woods to die.

Jack refused to search for Bobbie. He reasoned that the dog knew his time had come and he chose not to disturb his final resting place. A year earlier Bobbie was honoured by the Toronto Humane Society at its annual meeting. Jack could never bring himself to replace him with another pet.

He married in 1923 when he was 50. His wife, Lina, a Toronto concert soprano, was 10 years younger.

Jack Munroe died on February 12, 1942. He was 69. He is buried in his wife's family plot in Acton.

JACK Munroe was immortalized in "The Ballad of Jack Munroe," an anonymous piece of war poetry published in 1918. He was inducted in the Canadian Boxing Hall of Fame and he is an original member of Nova Scotia's Sport Hall of Fame.

NOVA SCOTIA GIANTS

ANGUS MCASKILL AND ANNA SWAN

I was noshing down on a smoked meat sandwich and a cherry Coke at Nate's deli in downtown Ottawa with two of my favourite characters – former MP and present dean of Canadian political columnists, Doug Fisher and former coach of Canada's national basketball team Jack Donohue.

I turned to Jack and said: "Let me ask you a whimsical, hypothetical question: "What would you give for the first born of two Nova Scotia giants, both over seven and a half feet tall? Your first born?"

Jack's flippant reply was: "My first born? I'd give my six born. No, I wouldn't. I'd encourage the giants to become suppliers to the National Basketball Association. They'd get paid more."

ANGUS "Giant" McAskill came to Canada with his parents from the outer Hebrides in 1828, when he was three years old.

He grew to be seven feet, nine inches tall and weighed 425 pounds. From his wrist to his fingertips, his hand measured 12 inches. He could pick up a pound of loose tea in one hand. He could carry a 300-pound barrel of pork under each arm.

The best-known photograph of "Giant" McAskill is a P. T. Barnum circus poster showing him with Tom Thumb standing in the palm of his hand. The photo is a hoax. Barnum superimposed a photo of the midget on McAskill's hand.

Giant McAskill's wife, Annie Potts, was over eight feet tall. Their bed was built from railroad ties.

Angus McAskill's dimensions were awesome. One of his half boots, currently in the provincial museum in Halifax, was fourteen and a half inches high, sixteen inches long and five inches wide.

His vest was sixty-two inches around and his Parisian beaver hat was seven and a half inches high and twenty-six and a half inches around the crown. He had an 80-inch chest.

Angus's father had to add an extension to his bed and raise the ceilings of the house.

ANNA Swan was born in Millbrook, Colchester County, but her family moved to Truro where she attended Truro Normal School. By the time she was six, she was as tall as her mother. At age 15, she was seven feet and at age 17 she was eight feet one inch.

Anna's husband, Captain Martin Van Buren Bates, was as tall as she was and outweighed her by 150 pounds. They had two children, but both died at birth. A daughter was 18 pounds at birth and a son weighed 28 pounds.

When Anna Swan was married in St. Martin-in-the-Fields church at Trafalgar Square on June 17, 1865, her wedding gown of 100 yards of satin and 50 yards of lace cost $1,000. Money was of little object, because showman P. T. Barnum was paying her $1,000 a month – later, $1,000 a week.

MCASKILL'S strength was prodigious. Once, he carried a very sick man 25 miles through a snowstorm and didn't set him down once. In a tavern in the United States he picked up a 140-gallon puncheon of Scotch whisky, rapped it with his knuckles until the bung flew out, and then raised the barrel to his lips and drank to the health of all those present.

Once, on a dare, he press-lifted an anchor that weighed 2,100 pounds, placed it on his shoulder, carried it a short distance and threw it on the beach.

His stool was fashioned from a 140-gallon molasses puncheon.

Giant McAskill and Anna Swan became sideshow freaks in Barnum's New York Broadway theatre. They shared billings with General Grant Jr., at 24 inches and 18 pounds the world's smallest living man; Tom Thumb; John Battersby, The Living Skeleton; his 742 pound wife, Hannah (she was twelve and a half times John's weight); and Jenny Lind.

McAskill and Swan toured Europe and were received by Queen Victoria, the Prince of Wales, crowned heads, dukes and princes. Victoria presented them with gold watches and diamond rings.

Giant McAskill came home to St. Ann's, Cape Breton, built a store overlooking the harbour and lived in it. Later, he bought a gristmill property at Munroe's Point, across from St. Ann's harbour.

Although a staunch Presbyterian, he declined to attend Sunday service because he disliked the congregation staring at him.

He died in St. Ann's on August 8, 1863. He was only 38. He was laid to rest in a hillside cemetery overlooking the

Englishtown ferry terminus. His original grave marker bore the inscription:

> Erected
> To
> The Memory of
> Angus McAskill
> Who died Aug. 8, 1863
> Aged 38 years
> A dutiful son, a kind brother,
> Just in all his dealings
> Universally respected by all his
> Acquaintance, "Mark the perfect
> Man, and behold the upright,
> For the end of that man is peace."

HIS original gravestone fell over, or was knocked over, and was reclaimed by nature. It was replaced with the current stone that has a slightly different inscription. Workmen uncovered the original stone years later and it is now an artifact in the Gaelic College at St. Ann's.

Anna Swan and her husband came back to North America in 1873. They bought a farm near Seville, Ohio. The house had 14-foot ceilings and door frames nine feet high. She was only 34 when she died in 1888. Her life-size statue stands over her grave in Mount Hill cemetery in Seville.

In Canada, she is remembered in Colchester County by the Anna Swan Museum, a small museum on the main street of Tatamagouche on Nova Scotia's Sunrise Trail.

MAD DOG KILLER
LESTER GILLIS

The Gillis family scratched out a living on a farm in Cape Breton's Margaree Valley. Some historical accounts refer to them as Highland Scot immigrants. Others claim that Josef and Mary Gillis were immigrants from Belgium who likely changed their surname to better blend in with their predominantly Scots-Irish neighbours.

Settling on a farm in Margaree in the late 1800s was a challenge. There were no roads or trails. Food, tools and personal effects had to be backpacked in. Broadaxes were the main tools to build a shelter. Land had to be cleared and stumps removed. Fields to be seeded were prepared with hoes and the seed was planted by hand. Crops were cut with sicles or reaping hooks and carried to the barn in sheaves. Grain was beaten from the straw with flails and ground for flour in hand mills.

Fig. 9. In their fabled history, the FBI only designated four criminals as Public Enemy Number One and two of them were Canadians. Lester Gillis, a.k.a. George Nelson, a.k.a. "Baby Face" Nelson was one. Courtesy FBI.

The Gillis family toughed it out for several winters, and decided there was a better life out there somewhere. The family moved to Chicago, but Josef Gillis had no illusions that Chicago's streets were paved with gold.

He found work as a packer at an icehouse on Canal Street at Union Stockyards. He worked 12 hours a day, six days a week.

A son, Lester Gillis, was born December 6, 1908, in Chicago in the Gillis's flat at 944 North California Street. He was an ill-tempered, spoiled brat. The Court TV crime library website described him as "something out of a bad dream. He was to emerge as one of the toughest and definitely the most heartless of Depression-era gangsters. Cold and brutal, he enjoyed killing. Even his criminal peers were wary of his path."

A crime reporter noted: "Where outlaws such as 'Pretty Boy' Floyd and the Barkers would kill to protect themselves when cornered, he went out of his way to murder – he loved it."

Author Robert Nash wrote in *Bloodletters and Badmen*: "His angelic pear-smooth face never betrayed his instant ability to kill."

Richard Lindberg, author of *Return to the Scene of the Crime*, wrote: "Standing only five feet, four inches, Gillis compensated for his physical limitations with a murderous temper and a willingness to employ a switchblade or a gun without hesitation or remorse for the intended victim."

Lester Gillis hunted with the hounds. He terrorized neighbourhood streets with a gang of juvenile hoodlums. At age fourteen, he was a veteran car thief. From there he graduated to stealing tires, running stills, bootlegging, armed robbery and murder.

Still only fourteen, he was convicted of auto theft and sent to reform school for two years. He was released on parole, but five months later he was back in for auto theft.

WHEN he was 23, he was sentenced to one year in Illinois State Prison for a January, 1931 Chicago bank robbery. While being transferred to Joliet Prison to stand trial for another bank robbery in Wheaton, Illinois, he escaped from his prison guards. It was the last time Lester would be in custody.

Lester fled to Sausalito, California, and then to Long Beach, Indiana and San Antonio, Texas. Along the way, he linked up with the Dillinger gang.

In 1933, a man was shot and killed in Minneapolis. The car used in the killing, bearing California plates, was traced back to Lester.

His next stop was Reno, Nevada. There, he killed a man who was a material witness in a United States mail fraud case.

IN APRIL, 1934, he went to Chicago and became a full-fledged member of the Dillinger gang. He vacationed with John Dillinger in northern Wisconsin.

The Federal Bureau of Investigation was tipped off that the gang was holed up at Little Bohemia Lodge. Barking dogs alerted the gangsters and they escaped in the darkness.

Gillis forced his way into a local home and took two hostages. Two FBI agents, J. C. Newman and W. Carter Baum, arrived with a local constable. Before their car had stopped rolling, the 133-pound Lester rushed it and ordered the three occupants out. He killed all three with his automatic pistol.

On June 30, 1934, Lester and John Dillinger robbed the Merchants National Bank in South Bend, Indiana. A police officer was shot and killed. Back in Chicago, Lester killed two more police officers who were closing in on the gang's hideout.

Dillinger was killed by FBI agents on July 22, 1934. Lester fled to California. En route, he was stopped for speeding in a small town. He paid a $5 fine at the police station and was allowed to proceed on his way. The car, containing rifles, Tommy guns and ammunition, was not searched.

Lester's trail of terror took him to Nevada, New York, Wisconsin and back to Chicago.

On November 27, 1934, two Chicago FBI agents spotted Lester driving a stolen car near Barrington, Illinois, and gave chase. Lester fired five shots from an automatic rifle and the agents returned fire. One shot pierced the radiator of Lester's car, disabling it.

FBI special agent Herman Edward Hollis was killed in the ensuing gun battle. FBI Inspector Samuel P. Cowley died from gunshot wounds a few hours later.

Lester was critically wounded by the fusillade of shots from the FBI agents. An accomplice helped him into the FBI agents' car and they drove off. Lester's body was found the next day near a Niles Center, Illinois, cemetery. He had 17 bullet holes in his body. One of the United States' most notorious gangsters and killers was dead — nine days before his 26th birthday.

In the annals of the Federal Bureau of Investigation only four men have been designated as Public Enemy Number One — John Dillinger, "Pretty Boy" Floyd, Canadian born Alvin "Creepy" Karpis and Lester Gillis.

Somewhere along the way, Lester Gillis changed his name to George Nelson, a prizefighter he admired.

The FBI knew Lester Gillis, a.k.a. George Nelson, the progeny of Margaree homesteaders, as "Baby Face" Nelson.

A GIANT OF A DIFFERENT SORT

M. M. COADY

Monsignor Moses Coady was a true Cape Breton giant. He stood six foot two and weighed 220 pounds.

His colleague and collaborator, Alex Laidlaw, wrote that his "giant stature ... made him look as though Rodin had hewn him, with a blunt chisel, out of granite rock. His stock in trade was ideas, simple but explosive ideas."

Someone once described M. M. Coady as looking like a cloned combination of heavyweight boxer Jack Dempsey and United Mine Workers President John L. Lewis.

The name Moses Coady appears on his birth certificate. Alex Laidlaw wrote that no one knew for sure what the other "M" stood for. Some thought Michael, others Mathias.

Coady was light-years ahead of some so-called futurists. He warned of "poisoning our earth and our waters" long before Rachel Carson's *Silent Spring*, her explosive volume on pollution.

He was an early advocate of research and development in industry, regional economic planning, scientific thinking and social change.

M. M. Coady was not afraid to ruffle feathers. He called for nuns to come out of their comfortable convents and mix in the ordinary workday lives of ordinary men and women. Shortly after his death in 1959, nuns marched in Selma, Alabama.

He was 25 years ahead of Pope John XXIII with regard to ecumenism. Alex Laidlaw wrote: "...he had been opening the windows of musty religious institutions many years before Pope John let fresh breezes blow through the Catholic Church."

The rumpled visionary warned: "There is a better life for all people. If we don't find a way to filter it down to them they will seek it in revolution, in communism."

The bluff priest feared no man – not even his Bishop, John R. MacDonald – who called him on the carpet in the Bishop's Palace in Antigonish. Bishop MacDonald upbraided Coady for including Protestant fisher folk in his social action mission in Guysborough County.

Coady looked down from his great height at the diminutive Bishop and replied: "Your Excellency, there is no Catholic or Protestant way to catch fish."

This came from the mouth of a gruff-talking priest who "by a fluke of destiny became identified with the fisheries and the fishermen." A couple of years earlier, he could hardly distinguish three species of fish.

Kingsley Brown, Southside Harbor, Antigonish County, relates a story that is part of the folklore of his Kinley in-laws' family.

"In the 1920s, Coady was campaigning against the introduction of steam trawlers. In Lunenburg, home of the great (Protestant to a man) schooner fleet, he stayed with the good Lutherans, Mr. and Mrs. J. J. Kinley.

"He was a wonderful man, a handsome man, Mrs. Kinley told me in the 1960s: 'He made marvelous speeches. He stayed with us, but I don't know if I'd let him in the house again. After dinner, he'd rest in

his room. He didn't take off his shoes and always left black polish on the bedspread.'

"The campaign to protect the hook-and-line fishery was successful. Canada limited the Atlantic fishery to three steam trawlers. The Europeans, with no restraints under international law, established their supremacy in the Atlantic fishery.

"Little Jimmy (Father Tompkins) was the heart of the (Antigonish) Movement, Coady the brains and the promoter."

MOSES Coady was born on a farm in the northeast Margaree Valley in 1882. He and Father Jimmy Tompkins were double first cousins. He worked on the modest but successful family farm until he enrolled in the Normal College in Truro in 1900.

He graduated in 1901 and became Principal of Margaree Forks School. He taught 15 subjects. Father Jimmy taught him Latin by correspondence. Coady entered St. FX University in 1903 and, two years later, had his Bachelor of Arts degree.

Next came studies at College Urbano, Rome, where he learned to speak Italian and earned a doctorate in philosophy. He was ordained a priest in 1910. In 1914-1915, he studied at Catholic University of America in Washington and was awarded a master's degree in education.

He returned to St. FX to teach philosophy and in 1925 he was named head of the education department.

In 1928, a Royal Commission on fisheries urged the organization of fisheries co-operatives. The Nova Scotia government hired Coady to undertake the task.

M. M. Coady had, at last, found a channel for his ideas and his energy, and he never looked back. So far as is known, he never worked as a curate or parish priest.

In 1928, St. FX's world famous extension department was created and Coady was named its director. The goal of the extension department was adult education and co-operatives in eastern Nova Scotia. Coady's vehicle was "social reform through economic acitivity."

Within a year, the United Maritime Fishermen's union was created.

Little did Coady dream that in the years to come, leaders from 120 nations would come to Antigonish to become immersed in the "Antigonish Movement." Coady gave Father Jimmy credit for the "movement." Between them, they were responsible for the United Maritime Fishermen and the Nova Scotia Teachers' Union.

He turned his considerable energy toward industrial Cape Breton and the plight of 12,000 coal miners who worked in dangerous conditions and were vastly underpaid by absentee "robber barons."

The coal company rented the miners and their families sub-standard housing – rows upon rows of double houses with no

bathrooms or toilets, no running water and foul smelling outhouses.

The company owned the stores where miners purchased their groceries and dry goods. The miners bought on credit and purchases were deducted from their Friday night pay envelopes. The stores were known as "pluck-me's."

The first Credit Union in Nova Scotia was opened in Reserve Mines in 1932. The first co-op housing group built their homes nearby and named the development "Tompkinsville." Co-op grocery and dry goods stores sprang up all over eastern Nova Scotia.

Coady persuaded fishermen to organize co-ops and market their catch together, saying: "…how do you think each one of you can go out into the world market with your little bundle of fish under your arm?"

He spoke the salty language of a fisherman. The old way of trying to go it alone was "like pissing up against a nor'wester."

Pope Pius appointed him Domestic Prelate – a Monsignor – in 1946.

M. M. Coady was in the winter of life when I was a student at St. FX, between 1952 and 1956. The extension department's office was in Xavier Hall, across the quadrangle from Morrison Hall where he had a small apartment.

He ate all his meals in the priests' dining room. He was a familiar figure on campus, shuttling between Xavier and Morrison Halls.

Father Gerald Roussel, now retired and living on campus in Mocker Hall, remembers Monsignor Coady fondly.

"He didn't smoke or drink. The only creature comfort he permitted himself was a game of bridge in the faculty lounge after dinner. He'd survey the dinner tables and mime shuffling cards. He was ready to play. Around 9 p.m. he'd start to doze off, so he'd go off to bed."

When illness forced Coady to step back in the 1950s, he was succeeded by another Cape Bretoner, Monsignor Michael J. MacKinnon – a.k.a. "Father Mike" or "Surly Mick."

"Surly Mick" was a private name he gave himself. He would survey a problem and say: "This looks like a job for Surly Mick, not Father Mike."

"Surly Mick" could be stern, tough and demanding.

It was left to Father Mike to square the circle. His analysis was that the extension department's program was weak in the field of agriculture. Eastern Co-op Services was born and provides over-all services to primary producers of Nova Scotia's eastern counties.

M. M. Coady left no worldly possessions. He gave everything away – gifts, money, books. A Protestant admirer who owned a clothing store provided most of what he wore. St. FX housed him and

fed him. People around the world who invited him to speak picked up all his expenses.

"What do I need money for, boy?" he would ask.

ONLY God knows how many fishing boats, nets, babies and college educations he financed.

He was given an early 1950s green Dodge or Plymouth car that he didn't like to drive. Usually, he would buttonhole a student and demand to be driven somewhere.

One morning, he grabbed my arm and told me he had to go to Sydney and that I was driving him. Who was I to argue against a day off classes?

The Canso Causeway was not yet a reality. We had to take a ferry across a Strait that was piled high with drift ice. Halfway across, the Monsignor got out of the car and stood on the deck to observe the ice breaking activity of the ferry.

The wind caught his snappy, new Homburg hat and it skimmed south, over the ice clampers like a black Frisbee.

All Coady said was: "F—k."

I was shocked. This innocent altar boy from St. Anne's Parish in Glace Bay had never heard a priest swear before.

WHEN it was required, he had the tongue of a longshoreman. But, inside was the soul of a poet. In 1949, he wrote *Masters of Their*

Own Destiny. It is still in print and has been translated into seven languages.

He wrote: "We have no desire to create a nation of shopkeepers, whose only thoughts run to groceries and dividends.

"We want our people to look into the sun, and into the depths of the sea. We want them to explore the hearts of flowers and the hearts of their fellow men. We want them to live, to love, to play and pray with all their being.

"We want them to be men, whole men, eager to explore all the avenues of life and to attain perfection in all their faculties. Life for them shall not be in terms of merchandising, but in terms of all that is good and beautiful, be it economic, cultural or spiritual.

"They are the heirs of all the ages and all the riches yet concealed. All the findings of science and philosophy are theirs. All the creations of art and literature are for them. If they are wise they will create the instruments to attain them. They will usher in a new day by attending to the blessings of the old."

Prose doesn't get much better than Coady's in *Masters of Their Own Destiny.*

Monsignor Moses Coady was laid to rest in 1959, in a graveyard high above the St. FX campus. Three months later, Monsignor Mike MacKinnon joined him.

POLITICAL KINGMAKER

FINLAY MACDONALD

Finlay MacDonald was one of few who made life in political backrooms rewarding – and fun. Politics was in the MacDonald genes.

Finlay's father, Finlay Sr., a Sydney lawyer, won three straight elections in Cape Breton South between 1925 and 1935.

Finlay Jr. was known in Sydney and at St. FX University as Ernie Finlay MacDonald.

By almost 5,000 votes, Finlay Sr. trounced Liberal heavyweight L. D. (Lauchie) Currie, the man who nominated Angus L. Macdonald for the Nova Scotia Liberal leadership and later served in his provincial cabinet.

He whipped populist Glace Bay Mayor Dan Willie Morrison by 2,500 votes. United Mine Workers' Labour candidate, Jim McLachlan, was snowed under by 5,700 votes.

Fig. 10. A most prized invitation from company president Brian Mulroney was one to the Iron Ore Company's private fishing camp in remote Labrador. Several times each Summer, Mulroney invited five friends to join him to try to outwit elusive Quebec "Reds" (large trout) with dry flies. Photo by Pat MacAdam.

In 1963, when his leadership was being buffeted, John Diefenbaker's close friends came to the aid of the party. Joel Aldred, a familiar face on every Canadian's TV set, ran against Mike Pearson in Algoma. Ottawa Roughrider all-star defensive back Joe Poirier took on Liberal heavyweight Paul Tardif. Newspaper baron John Bassett offered himself up as a *kamikaze* candidate in Toronto. Dick Thrasher resigned from his judge's bench to run in Windsor.

Finlay and veteran Tory MP Bob McCleave ran in the dual riding of Halifax against broadcaster Gerry Regan and Mayor Jack Lloyd and lost by 4,000 votes.

It was Finlay's only try for elected office. He spent the rest of his political life as a backroom kingmaker.

Finlay had it all – he was urbane, erudite, debonair, witty, had drop dead good looks, a prematurely silver brush cut, sartorial elegance, charm, wartime experience with the Cape Breton Highlanders, a successful Halifax radio career, governor of St. FX University, president of Industrial Estates, president of the Canadian Association of Broadcasters, Broadcast Hall of Fame. He was a board member of the Shaw Festival, president of

the highly successful Halifax-Dartmouth Canada Summer Games and the Order of Canada.

What does not appear in his c.v. is that he never took himself seriously – even when he was Bob Stanfield's main man in Halifax and his chief of staff in Ottawa.

Joe Clark passed him over for the Senate in 1979. During the week of the Diefenbaker funeral, Finlay was in Ottawa. I was Prime Minister Joe Clark's representative on the funeral organizing

Fig. 11. Finlay (centre) with former Prime Minister Brian Mulroney (left) and Sam Wakim, a Toronto lawyer and Mulroney's roommate at St. FX. Photo by Pat MacAdam.

committee. Finlay asked me to set up an appointment for him with Clark's appointments assistant, Jean Pigott. He was salivating for a senate seat.

I set up the appointment, but it was left to Brian Mulroney to appoint him to the senate in 1984 – Mulroney's very first Senate appointment.

In 13 years in the senate, Finlay was absent only 25 sitting days.

You had to get up very early to get ahead of Finlay MacDonald. One who did was Doug Harkness, a staffer at Finlay's Halifax radio station. Harkness did a perfect imitation of Bob Stanfield.

"Bob Stanfield" phoned Fin one evening and told him he was resigning as premier the next day. He said a scandal was brewing, that he had come home and found his wife in bed with a prominent Liberal.

"Who?"

"Ron Basford!" (Liberal Justice minister Ron Basford, Vancouver, he of wrestler "Gorgeous George's" flowing blond locks.)

With that, "Stanfield" hung up. Fin went ballistic. He spent the rest of the night trying to track the real Stanfield down.

Once, I managed to score a very minor plus in one-upmanship over Finlay. It was after an evening of door knocking in an Ottawa by-election. Janet and I were standing next to Bob Stanfield. The campaign manager announced

a whiparound and asked everyone to contribute generously.

When Fin opened his wallet, I said in a loud stage whisper to Bob Stanfield: "Did you see that, Mr. Stanfield, Finlay just opened his wallet and a moth flew out."

Travelling with Stanfield as his chief of staff, Fin had him kicked out of a first class lounge in Calgary. He told the Air Canada ground attendant: "That bald headed guy over there is not flying in first class. He's travelling economy. He shouldn't be in here."

On another occasion, Finlay, Stanfield and Amherst lawyer, businessman, "bagman" and eminence grise Rod Black were flying to Ottawa. Rod was a white-knuckle flyer and carried a small block of balsa wood and a penknife in his vest pocket. He whittled to calm his nerves.

Finlay told the stewardess that Rod was mentally disturbed and was being taken to an insane asylum near Ottawa: "We think he has a knife. For Christ's sake, don't give him anything to drink."

Rod's tongue was hanging down past his ankles when the flight touched down in Ottawa.

In 1963, the wheels fell off John Diefenbaker's war wagon. Defence Minister Douglas Harkness, of Calgary, resigned from cabinet over nuclear tips for Bomarc missiles. We were at a national campaign committee meeting in a west end Ottawa motel, when Dalton Camp and Eddie

Fig. 12. Left to right: Jim McGrath, former St. John's, Newfoundland, MP, Joe Clark's Minister of Fisheries and Newfoundland's Lieutenant Governor; Finlay MacDonald; Iron Ore Company of Canada President Brian Mulroney; Pat MacAdam; Sam Wakim and St. FX classmate and Mayor of Pembroke, Ontario, lawyer Terry McCann. Courtesy Pat MacAdam.

Goodman told us George Hees and Pierre Sevigny were on their way to 24 Sussex to resign.

What to do? Last one out – turn out the lights!

The 30 bagmen, organizers, cabinet ministers and senators hastily cobbled a resolution of support for The Chief's continued leadership. We trooped down to 24 Sussex in an army of taxicabs.

The Chief received us on crutches. He had sprained an ankle when he stepped in a groundhog hole at the prime minister's summer residence at Harrington Lake, Quebec.

Suddenly, Finlay was spokesman for the group.

Who appointed Finlay?

"Prime Minister, your national campaign committee has just passed a unanimous resolution supporting you – with one proviso."

What was Finlay up to? There were no provisos.

Dief's eyes shot out like organ stops and his nostrils flared. I thought he was going to impale Finlay on a crutch. I was looking for a window to go through or a likely spot in the wall to make a new door.

"What's that," Dief bellowed?

Unflappable Finlay didn't flinch.

He said: "Prime Minister, we want your solemn promise that between now and the next election – you won't step in any more gopher holes."

Finlay's finest hour had to be that night in 1979 when Prime Minister Joe Clark's closest advisors huddled at 24 Sussex Drive. It was a damage control session following Clark's bonehead announcement that the Canadian Embassy in Tel Aviv, Israel, was being moved to Jerusalem.

The firestorm of public protest was intense. The excrement hit the rotating overhead ventilating device at high speed.

Clark's brain trust decided to try to defuse the issue by buying time – sending Bob Stanfield off to the Middle East on a six-week "fact finding" mission. An Order-in-Council would appoint him plenipotentiary extraordinary.

Finlay arrived late for the meeting at 24 Sussex and it was obvious he had had a few drams of Highland single malt.

He was apprised of the group's plan and told it was "saucered and blown."

Then, the other shoe was dropped. They wanted Finlay to go see Stanfield and persuade him to accept the commission.

Finlay exploded in mock outrage: "You want me to go and see the finest prime minister Canada never had and ask him to spend six weeks in the desert in 125 degree heat?

"You want me to persuade the man who came within two seats of toppling the Trudeau government and forming one of his own?

"You want me to go and see the man who led Nova Scotia conservatives out of the wilderness after 23years of liberal rule?

"You want me to lean on the best premier Nova Scotia ever had?

"You want me to talk to Bob Stanfield and ask him to do one more for the gipper?

"You want me to intrude on a longstanding friendship with a man who lost his first wife in a tragic auto accident and a second wife to a horrible death from cancer?

"Now that he has happily remarried to Anne, you want me to go to their ivy-covered honeymoon home on Acacia Avenue in Rockcliffe. I'll walk in and there will be the loving couple, in front of a roaring fire, entwined together on a bearskin rug, stark naked and bonking their brains out.

"You want me to trespass on that?"

Finlay had class.

He had style.

WHEN his time was up in the Senate – he turned 75 – senators Norm Atkins, John Lynch-Staunton, Al Graham, John Buchanan, Joyce Fairbairn, Sharon Carstairs and others heaped praise on Finlay's contribution.

Al Graham recalled his own time in 1958 when he was the (unsuccessful) Liberal standard bearer in Antigonsh-Guysbrough. Finlay was one of the main bagmen in Nova Scotia. The day before the election, Fin arrived in Antigonish with a significant amount of cash for Al's Tory opponent, Angus R. MacDonald – "enough to do me in," recalled Senator Graham.

Fin wasn't looking forward to mandatory retirement from the senate when he turned 75. In all seriousness, he asked Janet: "Where am I going to get a job when I retire? Who's going to hire a 75 year-old"?

Finlay passed away in 2002 with a life still in progress. He was 79.

DATE WITH THE HANGMAN

DR. ISADORE GOLD

A military doctor saved the life of Japan's wartime prime minister Hideki Tojo, who had a date with the hangman. That doctor was Glace Bay native Captain Isadore Gold.

A few days after Japan surrendered, a half-dozen American vehicles encircled Tojo's house. Japan's wartime leader looked out from an open window and asked if they had a warrant for his arrest.

When he was advised they did have a warrant, he placed a .32 calibre pistol to his chest and pulled the trigger. He missed his heart by a fraction of an inch. A Japanese doctor who examined him said his condition was "hopeless." He guessed that Tojo wanted to die like a soldier – not at the end of a rope on the gallows.

Captain Isadore Gold was a Canadian doctor serving with a U.S. medical unit. He immediately administered a life saving transfusion of plasma from a Canadian source. It is difficult to corroborate, but sources reported that the plasma came from blood donated by a Canadian RCAF serviceman from Halifax.

Tojo lived to face a war crimes trial and death by hanging.

ISADORE Gold was born in Glace Bay, graduated from Morrison Glace Bay High School and received his medical degree from Dalhousie University. He served as a pathologist at Montreal General Hospital before transferring to Brooklyn Jewish Hospital in New York.

Dr. Gold enlisted in the U.S. Army and served with a MASH unit that island-hopped with American forces across the Pacific. He was among the first physicians to enter the ruins of Nagasaki after the U.S. dropped a second atomic bomb.

Tojo had once said the definition of war criminal depended on whether one was a winner or a loser. When Japan surrendered unconditionally on August 15, 1945, Tojo was a loser. He waited in his simple garden at home for the victors to come and try him as a war criminal.

He was then just Hideki Tojo, private citizen and army general on the retired list. He drew a standard army pension and lived modestly in a small Tokyo home. For all intents and purposes, Tojo was unemployed.

From October 1941, to June 25, 1944, however, he was prime minister, war minister, armaments minister, education minister and Chief of the Imperial Japanese General Staff. He was dismissed by Emperor Hirohito on June 25, 1944.

Tojo was an unlikely looking warlord. He stood five-feet tall and was slight of build. American editorial cartoonists took delight in portraying him as an evil, buck-toothed monkey and he was seen in cartoons and propaganda posters hanging from a tree by his tail with his Axis partners Adolf Hitler and Benito Mussolini.

Tojo was also an unlikely military chess master – the architect of most of Japan's military setbacks. He was jealous of successful military commanders and had them banished to the rear echelons. His most brilliant tactician, Admiral Yamamoto, was killed when his transport plane was shot down by American Lockheed Lightning planes.

As the U.S. war machine grew stronger, General Douglas MacArthur's promise – "I shall return" – took on an air of credibility. The American campaign of island hopping was driving Japanese forces back towards their home islands.

Allied landings on Saipan, which began on June 15, 1944, were the end for Tojo. The Japanese garrison had no air support. The U.S. managed to land three entire divisions on the island the first day of the assault.

On June 25, Emperor Hirohito convened a body that had never met before – *Gensui-In* – the board of field marshals and fleet admirals. The situation was fast becoming intolerable; officers and men on Saipan had not eaten for three days.

The Emperor was convinced the war had to be ended and that Prime Minister Hideki Tojo must go.

The Emperor dismissed Tojo as prime minister and stripped him of all other cabinet offices. Tojo's entire cabinet resigned.

Tojo cleaned out his desk in the Diet Building and moved out of his official residence. He and his wife, Kasuko, moved back to their house in Tokyo's suburbs.

His July 18 fall from grace and power was, in one way, a stroke of luck, for his enemies had planned to assassinate him with a bomb laced with potassium cyanide, to be delivered to the prime minister's office July 20.

The plot was cancelled.

TOJO raised chickens for their eggs. He grew vegetables to supplement Tokyo's scant food supply. He did some writing. During the summer of 1945, flames from bombs dropped by American B-29s destroyed his home.

He refused to move: "I have to remain here. The Emperor may call on me."

Tojo knew the war was over. He knew he would be put on trial and he knew what the outcome of the trial would be. He asked a neighbour, Dr. Suzuki, to show him the exact location of his heart.

He planned to take his own life if capture was imminent, but he was not prepared to commit suicide until he saw which way the wind was blowing. He planned to use a pistol rather than the traditional samurai sword to commit *seppuku*.

GENERAL Tojo was almost alone in the prisoners' dock at his war crimes trial. There was strong Allied pressure to put Emperor Hirohito on trial, especially from Russia. General Douglas MacArthur, military governor of the occupying forces, reasoned the Emperor would be more valuable to him alive as his puppet than dead as a god-like martyr.

Many of Japan's top military leaders chose to take their own lives – Prince Konoye; Admiral Matome Ugali, who had been in command of air defence for the home islands; General Anami,

Tojo's successor as war minister; Field Marshal Sugiyama, who feared war crimes retribution for Doolittle bomber raids and prisoners of war in Malaya and Dutch East Indies; General Shirokura; and Admiral Takejiro, who was responsible for the formation of *kamikaze* suicide squadrons.

Tojo stood trial with five other generals and one civilian, Koki Hiroto, former prime minister and foreign minister.

The outcome of the trial was a foregone conclusion – death by hanging – a form of execution repugnant to Japanese culture. Tojo refused to allow his lawyers to file an appeal.

At midnight, December 23, 1948, the seven were to be hanged to satisfy the victors' thirst for vengeance.

Tojo's last request – a Japanese meal and a cup of *sake* rice wine for the seven condemned – was refused.

Tojo and three generals were first to die. Before they mounted the thirteen steps to the hangmen's nooses, they were permitted a short visit to a shrine where they lit incense sticks. Standing on the gallows traps they gave three cheers for the Emperor.

The nooses were adjusted, black hoods were placed over their heads and ninety seconds after midnight they dropped into eternity. Their remains were cremated immediately and the ashes co-mingled to discourage neo-samurai groups from using the ashes as symbols of martyrdom.

The ashes were then thrown into a swift flowing river.

After the war, General Tojo's widow presented Dr. Isadore Gold with her husband's ceremonial sword as a gesture of gratitude.

DR. GOLD returned to the United States and resumed his medical practice at Brooklyn Jewish Hospital. He switched his medical practice from pathology to obstetrics and gynecology.

He passed away in New York on April 19, 1996. His widow lives in New York and still has Tojo's ceremonial sword.

BOUND FOR GLORY

EDDIE SWARTZACK

Fig. 13. Eddie Swartzack, Montreal Nationales winger (far right), stick raised high, signals his goal against Quebec Citadels on March 14, 1952, in Game #5 of the Quebec Junior League playoffs. Montreal won 4-2. Citadels trailed Montreal in games 3-0 and 4-2 but rallied to tie the series 4-4 and won the deciding ninth game 3-2 when a Quebec defenceman scored with 59 seconds left in the game. Photographer unknown. Photo courtesy of Eddie Swartzack

The blonde kid from Glace Bay arrived in Montreal in September 1951. A virtual unknown walk-on at Canadiens training camp, the eighteen year-old left winger soon ignited a bidding war for his services.

Phil Watson salivated over him for his Quebec Citadels, but wanted to convert him to defence. Montreal Nationales coach Pete Morin wanted him. Morin followed him around with a blank contract, even followed him to Quebec City and stole him out from under Watson.

The *Hockey News* noted that the Nationales were "strengthened by the addition of Ed Swalzhad [*sic*] from Glace Bay."

That was the last time a Quebec journalist would misspell the name of Eddie Swartzack, who set the Quebec Major Junior League on fire with his electrifying play.

He scored 29 goals and added 39 assists in 50 games. He was voted Rookie of the Year. He missed making the first all-star team by one vote, he and coach Morin being voted to the second team.

The league's six coaches selected Eddie as the "league's best professional prospect." Coaches could not vote for members of their own teams.

At first, opposing players ran at the rookie from Glace Bay, but they soon learned the 165 pounds on a five foot eleven frame was hard as nails, could hit back and did.

Montreal Star writer Charlie Boire wrote, late in the 1951-52 season: "He has yet to turn in a bad game."

Hap Emms, owner-coach of the Barrie Flyers, doffed his hat to Eddie: "That guy is the best junior player in the Quebec League," who had just turned a hat-trick in a 6-4 win over Barrie in the Montreal Forum.

Junior Canadiens' coach Sam Pollock offered Nationales' general manager Emile "Butch" Bouchard five players for Swartzack.

NHL teams were allowed to bring up two juniors for three-game tryouts. The Canadiens brought up Jean Beliveau and placed Eddie on "stand-by" in the event a starting Canadien was injured.

Baz O'Meara, the dean of Montreal sportswriters, pronounced in his *Montreal Star* column: "Here is a future great."

A year later, "the mirror crack'd."

Fig. 14. *Eddie Swartzack, suited up with the Montreal Nationales. Photographer unknown. Courtesy Pat MacAdam.*

ON January 15, 1953, Eddie's 20th birthday, doctors told him he had tuberculosis. He caught the disease from a roomer in a boarding house. He spent the next nine months in a TB hospital in east-end Montreal. (The hospital is long gone and the 1976 Olympic Village stands on the site.)

Only Canadiens general manager Frank Selke and Sam Pollock came to visit him. His teammates dared not risk being exposed to the highly contagious disease.

Although the Canadiens looked after all his medical expenses and gave him $125 a month spending money, his boyhood dream of playing in the NHL was cruelly taken away from him.

"Sam Pollock also gave me a club blazer with the Canadiens' crest and I still have it in a closet somewhere," Eddie said.

The fire that burned intensely in Eddie's belly was lit when he was "ten or twelve."

Every chance we had we played on bogs, marshes and rivers and on the street. When we had ice time at the Glace Bay Miners' Forum, we'd be waiting at the door for the rink staff to open up. We used to listen to Foster Hewitt on the radio on Saturday nights. The players were just names to me. I didn't start putting faces to them until I joined the Canadiens' organization. During workouts, I found myself trying to get by Doug Harvey or trying to put a puck past Gerry MacNeil.

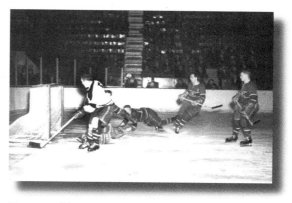

Fig. 15. Eddie scores against Charlie Hodge (future Vezina Trophy winner with the NHL's Montreal Canadiens), in nets for the Junior Canadiens. Photographer unknown. Courtesy Ed Swartzack.

"Another bonus was the cheap $1.25 rush seats at the Montreal Forum. I could see the best players in action but, more importantly, I could learn from their moves."

Eddie was standing at the end of the rink the night Scotty Bowman's hockey career ended. Scotty was on a breakaway when Three Rivers defenceman Jean-Guy Talbot hit him with a two-handed chop on the back of his head. The life threatening injury left Bowman with a silver plate in his skull. Talbot was suspended.

Eddie played minor hockey in Glace Bay with St. John's CYO on a line with his brother Gene and Jackie "Lily" MacLellan. The entire line enrolled at St. FX and proceeded to re-write the record books

– two Maritime intercollegiate titles and two Maritime senior crowns.

In 1949-1950, the trio from Glace Bay scored 61 goals in 30 games and shared 56 assists; Eddie had 32 goals.

The next season he scored 60 times and assisted on 47 goals in 50 games. His line accounted for 135 goals and 238 points. He was 17.

Eddie's team went on to represent the Maritimes in Allan Cup quarter-finals, but were eliminated, St. FX winning but one game – Eddie scored a hat trick.

St. FX was short-listed to represent Canada in the 1952 Olympics in Oslo, Norway, but were edged out by the Edmonton Mercurys.

Montreal columnist Andy O'Brien plumped for St. FX in *Weekend Magazine*. He wrote that "St. FX was probably the only amateur team in Canada; the players provide their own skates and incidental equipment."

THEN it was time for Eddie to spread his wings. His old coach at St. John's CYO, Father Frank MacNeil, forwarded a packet of press clippings to Frank Selke and advised him that he was driving Eddie Swartzack to Montreal. Eddie who?

"We stopped over in Boston and took in a ball game at Fenway Park, Eddie recalled. Father MacNeil drove me the rest of the way to Montreal and then headed back home."

Eddie was assigned to the Nationales who played in the six-team Quebec junior league (the Canadiens owned all or part of four teams). The Quebec Citadels were a New York Rangers farm team.

Coach Morin offered Eddie $45 a week but, with Morin's blessing, Eddie went over his head and negotiated directly with Frank Selke. Eddie left Selke's office with a handshake and a solid gold contract for $2,500 for the five-month season.

Nationales drew Quebec Citadels in a best-of-nine semifinal series. Citadels were down three games to none and four games to two, but tied the series at four. The final game was in Quebec Coliseum before 15,000 fans. A Citadel defenceman scored with 59 seconds remaining to give Quebec a 3-2 win and the series.

Eddie's father, Freeman, was a coal miner in Glace Bay. Eddie sent him money to come up for the series with the Citadels.

"The Canadiens treated him like royalty and he watched the games from box seats," said Eddie.

The Nationales were disbanded and Eddie was assigned to the Montreal Royals, then to the Junior Canadiens and the senior Royals. The Junior Royals won the Memorial Cup in 1949-1950, but half the team had been traded to the Nationales, who won only six of 42 games in 1950-1951 and won three and tied two in 50 games in 1951-1952. Eddie Swartzack joined the Royals and was expected to lead them out of the wilderness "proving ground" of the Canadiens.

The Royals won two and tied two of their first 25 games and then went winless in 15 games. Despite playing for the league's basket case, Eddie was a strong contender for the scoring title. But, crashing into the boards in a game against the Toronto Marlboros put him out of action for two weeks.

At the time, Henri Richard and Bobby Rousseau were atop the pile with 39 points each. Claude Provost was next with 34 points and Eddie had 28.

Just before the trade deadline, Eddie was dealt to the Junior Canadiens. The *Montreal Star* reported: "It took him about five minutes to adapt himself to the Canucks' style of play and he was away."

Eddie was the darling of Montreal sportswriters. They couldn't get enough of him. The *Star*'s Fred Roberts wrote: "The only way to stop Swartzack is to keep him in a straitjacket. The Glace Bay native plays practically 45 minutes of a game – he is used on other lines and as a roving defenceman."

At various times, Charlie Boire of the *Star* wrote: "He was on the puck so much it began to look like part of his boot heel.

"...there is another star from the east appearing on the horizon who should be in the big tent in a few short years.

"...a tireless two-way worker who is always a dangerous threat.

"...he is used to kill penalties, work on power plays and does the odd stint on defence.

"Pete Morin, a good judge of hockey talent, tabbed Swartzack for stardom the first time he lamped him in practice.

"Swartzack has been the sparkplug behind Nationales all season.

"... rugged Ed.

"The Glace Bay bullet is an unassuming lad and his popularity with his teammates and fans is easily understandable.

"... by far the outstanding man on the ice.

"Swartzack, who was a one-man team, salted away the game with his third goal and what proved to be the winner."

Other sportswriters called him "Steady" Eddie.

AND then, the music stopped. His hockey career was over. The doctors at the TB hospital recommended six to eight months in the sun in Arizona. Arranging it, Frank Selke wrote: "I have never sent you any boy who has as many good qualities as Eddie Swartzack."

But, Eddie had other plans. Instead of making a right turn for Arizona, he hung a left and returned to St. FX for a commerce degree. He graduated in May 1956, and he and Delores Boudreau were married the following Saturday. Following a brief honeymoon, he joined Revenue Canada where he worked for 33 years—half in Halifax and half in Ottawa.

Their daughter, Cindy, was a member of Canada's national diving team and represented Canada at the international championships in Stuttgart.

A CYNICAL old Ottawa pro who played five NHL seasons and who won the Calder Rookie of the Year Trophy, caustically volunteered: "Maybe the illness was a blessing in disguise. He never would have made any money playing pro hockey."

THE "UNKNOWN KID"

JOHNNY MILES

The Boston Marathon, the world's oldest annual marathon, is run in April on Patriot's Day in Massachusetts.

Some historians believe the name marathon is named after the 490 BC Battle of Marathon when Pheidippides ran 150 miles to Sparta in two days to bring news of a Greek victory over the Persians. He reported: "Rejoice, we are victorious" and fell dead.

The modern race distance was determined in the 1908 London Olympics. The distance from the starting line at Windsor Castle, where King Edward VII saw the runners off, to the finish line in London was 26 miles, 385 yards.

Today, the Boston Marathon field has been limited to 15,000 runners. A record number – 38,708 – took part in the 100th running in 1996.

Nineteen-year old Johnny Miles shocked the sporting world in 1926 when he won the very first competitive marathon he ever ran – in 2:25:40. He ran against the world's best and won, demolishing world and Boston records.

He was already in the shower when Olympic and world champion Albin Stenroos of Finland finished second – four minutes behind him. American runner Clarence DeMar, Olympic bronze medal winner, finished a distant third.

The unknown grocery delivery boy, down from his horse drawn wagon, destroyed Stenroos's 1924 Olympic and world record of 2:41:22 by almost 16 minutes.

A Boston newspaper banner headline of April 20, 1926, read:

"Unknown kid smashes record in greatest of all marathons"

HIS record stood until 1948, when it was broken by a Korean runner.

Fig. 16. Two-time winner of the Boston Marathon, Johnny Miles poses with the silverware he won as an amateur marathon runner in the world's top marathons and Commonwealth and Olympic Games. Photographer unknown. Courtesy Floyd Williston and the late Dr. John Miles Williston.

The "unknown kid" ran his first ever marathon wearing cheap 98¢ canvas sneakers purchased from the local co-op store in Florence, Cape Breton, where the Miles family settled when they emigrated from Britain. His home-sewn jersey featured a red Maple Leaf with "N.S." superimposed in white.

Before leaving Cape Breton for Boston, he took a train 27 miles out of town and ran back along the tracks in freezing weather and slippery snow and slush. Two hours and 40 minutes later he was home. It was his very first marathon run. He was ready.

The townspeople of Florence passed the hat and collected $300 – the equivalent of three months' pay – to send the Miles family to Boston. When they arrived, Johnny and his father walked the entire length of the course so that he might familiarize himself with the landmarks, twists and turns, and ups and downs of the route.

Boston opened its large heart to Johnny and his parents. They had intended to take a train home the day after the race, but ended staying for a week of red carpets, police motorcycle escorts, receptions and media attention. The mayor gave Johnny the key to the city.

He set out to defend his title in 1927, but was forced to drop out after six miles, his feet bleeding badly. Tar, softened by a temperature in the 80s, was oozing into his flimsy sneakers. He went back in 1929, won again, and set another world and Boston record.

He went back to Boston one more time in 1931 and finished a disappointing 10th— 18 minutes behind the winner.

HE RAN for Canada in the 1928 Amsterdam and 1932 Los Angeles Olympics and, even though he posted respectable times, he finished 16th and 14th. The last hurrah for Johnny Miles was near.

In 1930 he was a bronze medalist in the first ever British Empire Games held in Hamilton.

MARATHONER Ken Doucette, who recently moved from Ottawa to Halifax, is another player in the small freemasonry of marathon runners who kept in touch with Miles. Doucette had mixed emotions when

he broke his hero's 54-year old Nova Scotia marathon record in a New Orleans Mardi Gras race.

"When I broke his record in 1980, Johnny Miles was the first person to call me and congratulate me, Doucette recalls.

"Johnny Miles was a natural athlete who never had access to elite coaching or training and who didn't even own a proper pair of running shoes. Who knows? I think if he had a good coach and trainer and proper footwear, he might have been capable of turning in a 2:10 marathon back in the 20s."

Johnny Miles' family had a hardscrabble life in a Cape Breton coal mining town. When his father went off to war, 11-year old Johnny became the bread winner. He cleaned miners' lamps for 35¢ a day until he landed a better job paying $15 a week. Every Friday he gave his unopened pay envelope to his mother and she gave him a 25¢ allowance. Some weeks she was forced to ask for the 25¢ back to buy groceries.

When World War II broke out, Johnny was too old to enlist and spent the war building Bren Gun carriers in International Harvester's Hamilton Ontario plant. For the next 25 years he worked for International Harvester in increasingly responsible executive positions in Hamilton, Europe and the United States. While in Chicago, 50-year old Johnny earned a Master's degree in Business Administration.

Throughout his running career he was a true amateur. His feats over 15 years did not net him a single penny – neither victor's spoils nor appearance money. His only pay day was when he was 17 and entered a local three-mile race. One prize was a 98-pound bag of flour donated by a town grocer. The first runner past the grocer's store at the midpoint of the race would win it. His mother needed flour, so he made sure he was first by the store. He finished the race in third place.

When the 25th annual Johnny Miles Memorial Marathon was run in New Glasgow, the winning time was eight minutes slower than Johnny Miles's 1926 record.

A NATURAL DELIVERY

DANNY GALLIVAN

Cape Breton's best known Irishman, Danny Gallivan wasn't much of a hockey buff when he was a teenager. His older brother, the late Monsignor Bill, remarked: "His first love was baseball. He was attracted to it as metal is to a magnet."

From Whitney Pier, Danny was probably the best baseball pitcher Nova Scotia has ever produced. Between 1932 and 1938, he pitched Sydney junior, intermediate and senior teams to an unequalled skein of provincial, regional and national titles.

Just how good was he?

The New York Giants won league pennants in 1936 and 1937 (but lost both World Series to the Yankees). In 1938, Danny was invited to attend the Giants' tryout camp in Baton Rouge. He rubbed shoulders with Giants greats Mel Ott and Carl Hubbell.

Ott hit 511 home runs in 22 seasons. Between 1932 and 1937, Hubbell posted five consecutive 20-plus game winning seasons; 115 wins, 22 saves and a stingy 2.54 earned run average.

Danny Gallivan and Danny Seaman from Liverpool were among 139 rookies. They were picked as the two most promising prospects in camp. Gallivan's scouting report indicated he had the "best fastball and best curve ball." Seaman's report described him as the "hardest and most consistent batter."

"Seaman is a natural batter. Gallivan has a natural delivery. He throws smoke," the scouts' jottings revealed.

In his first appearance in the big league, Danny Gallivan pitched the first three innings and held opposition batters hitless. He struck out five and walked one. Shortstop Seaman went three for four at the plate.

The Giants had good news and bad news for the two Dannys. The good news

Fig.17. 1936 Whitney Pier Amateur Baseball Club. Danny Gallivan is seated front row at far left. In the second row, third from the left, is his older brother Fr. William Gallivan. Photo by Dodge. Courtesy Gary Gallivan, Whitney Pier Museum.

Danny Gallivan was scouted by the New York Giants and invited to their try-out camp. He was rated a "top prospect" and the scouting and coaching reports indicated he "throws smoke." But the reports also warned that the fastball pitcher was in danger of injuring his shoulder and arm. Danny heeded the advice, gave up thoughts of a pro career and enrolled at St. FX.

was they were offered contracts with a farm team – Milford, Delaware, of the Eastern Shore League. Danny Gallivan would have pitched to future all stars and hall of famers Phil Rizzuto and Sid Gordon.

The bad news was that Danny's arm and shoulder were severely damaged.

Giants trainers told him if he continued to throw hard he might "end up disabled." His cousin, Gary Gallivan, Whitney Pier Museum curator, guesses his arm was burned out because he pitched too often when his body was still developing.

It wasn't "Spahn and Sain and two days of rain," Danny pitched every game.

He returned to Nova Scotia and enrolled at St. Francis Xavier University. Hollywood director Dan Petrie, his college roommate and lifelong friend, recalls: "Danny was quite famous in Nova Scotia. I remember reading about him on an almost daily basis during baseball seasons in 1936 and 1937.

"I know that when I got to St. FX, I was in a registration line and he was in front of me. I saw his name on a notebook and I reacted like a goofy fan: 'Wow, are you the real Danny Gallivan'?"

Dan Petrie and Danny Gallivan went off to war in Europe. Dan was badly injured in a motorcycle crash, invalided home and spent a year in hospital while his body healed.

The Gallivans were a large clan with thirteen children. The oldest, Bill, entered the priesthood and was named Domestic Prelate – a Monsignor – by the Pope. He was also Vicar General, second-in-command to the Bishop of Antigonish. Another older brother, Wilfred, served in the United States merchant marine and was murdered in Spain in 1948.

Danny's father, Luke, worked as a shipper-trimmer on the coal piers. A trimmer was responsible for ensuring the cargo was balanced in a ship's hold.

DANNY'S broadcasting career began at CJFX, Antigonish, while he attended university. After graduation he taught high school algebra and Latin and did some hockey and baseball broadcasts.

In 1946, he became sports director of CJCH, Halifax.

CBC hockey producer Walter Downs heard Danny's play-by-play of a Memorial Cup game between Halifax St. Mary's and Montreal. He tucked the name and the voice away in his memory bank.

In 1950, the Montreal Canadiens' play-by-play broadcaster, Doug Smith, suffered a mild heart attack. In 1952, he elected to give up hockey for a less demanding gig as voice of the Montreal Alouettes. Downs remembered the urbane Nova Scotian with the golden tones and called him up from the farm to the big show.

When he switched off his microphone 32 years later, Danny had called more than 1,800 NHL games. He was the ironman of sports broadcasters; 22 years went by before he missed a game, through illness, in 1974.

His Halifax friend, sportswriter Pat Connolly, says: "Foster Hewitt created the art of hockey broadcasting, but Danny refined it to a degree and a standard that I doubt will ever be equalled."

DAN Petrie delivered the eulogy at Danny's funeral in 1993. He said: "Danny not only vividly described hockey games, he managed to make each broadcast an

English lesson. Danny introduced at least one new word each game. He suited up the English language and sent it out to centre ice."

Serge Savard didn't wheel at the blueline; he executed a "Savardian spin-a-rama."

Bobby Orr didn't just lug the puck; he led a "scintillating rush."

Doug Harvey didn't just unload a slap shot; he "unleashed a cannonading drive."

Even though my mother was a Gallivan and Danny's second cousin, I didn't meet him until I was 30. I worked in the PR department of Expo 67 and Danny and I lunched often at the Montreal Press Club.

One noon, Mordecai Richler and Montreal Gazette sports columnist-lawyer "Dink" Carroll joined us. Mordecai steered the conversation onto Danny's superb command of English and his patented "Gallivanisms."

Danny chuckled. He told us that every time he announced that so-and-so fired a "howitzer" shot, he heard from a nit-picking English professor "probably with a military background." The professor wouldn't let up. He'd write, fax or phone to remonstrate that Danny's use of "howitzer" was inappropriate. A "howitzer" shell arrives at its objective "in a parabolic trajectory." A cannon delivers its payload in a straight line.

When I returned to Ottawa we kept in touch. Danny would always come up with

Forum tickets for my two young sons and me. But I was reluctant to ask because he would never accept payment. He always insisted we come up to the broadcast booth before a game to say hello. He introduced my boys to Canadiens' greats – Doug Harvey, Jean Beliveau, Dickie Moore – but by this time, the little traitors had stepped out of their father's shadow. Bobby Orr was their idol.

Danny's other passion was politics – Liberal party politics. He was mentioned frequently as a federal Liberal candidate in industrial Cape Breton. His son, Danny Jr., QC, a Halifax lawyer with a Tory law firm, told me his father looked at Cape Breton South and riding Liberals commissioned a poll.

Danny Jr. says the poll was unfavourable and his father backed off. He had been away from Cape Breton too long and he would have had to square off with a popular incumbent, coal miner Donnie MacInnis, who held the riding from 1957 until he retired in 1979. (MacInnis lost the riding to the NDP in 1962, but regained it in 1963.)

Danny was named to every hall of fame the worlds of sport, hockey and broadcasting have to offer. The Canadiens named the Forum pressbox "Passerelle Lecavalier-Gallivan" after Rene Lecavalier and Danny. When he retired, he became a goodwill ambassador for Hockey Night in Canada. His broadcast colleague, Dick

Irvin, says that every time Danny appeared in person at an event: "I don't care how many athletes were there, who the big stars were from hockey, football, whatever – if Danny Gallivan was at the head table, he was the star of the show."

In a 1972 interview, Danny was critical of NHL expansion, he felt had moved so quickly that "hockey has very noticeably diluted in calibre." Among other intelligent insights, he expressed the wish that the Stanley Cup champions play the Soviet champions.

Was Danny a prophet 30 years ago? Anyone who has watched the incredibly fast and clean hockey played during the Olympics must agree that he was. He believed regular seasons were too long and too many teams made the playoffs. He favoured larger ice surfaces where "the truly skilled players would excel" and "there would be less hooking and slashing."

Danny died in his sleep in his Nuns' Island apartment in Montreal in 1993. He was 75. He had just returned from a golfing trip in the Carolinas. His brother, Pat, says: "He was in pretty good health but I guess it was his heart … just died off in his sleep – that's the way mother went."

He is remembered at St. FX. Friends and hockey acquaintances established a scholarship fund in his name and the principal now stands at more than $250,000. The interest is used for athletic scholarships, which more than cover annual tuition fees.

The broadcasting legend was buried in Montreal. Monsignor Bill Gallivan celebrated the Requiem Mass. Danny's friend, Denis Ryan, an Irish folk-singer with Halifax's Ryan's Fancy, ended the service with the Irish ballad "Danny Boy." There were 500 mourners in St. Ignatius Loyola church in Montreal. Back in Cape Breton, 750 friends and relatives remembered him at a service in his old parish church, Holy Redeemer.

The Whitney Pier Legion's bugler sounded the last post and a bagpiper played "Flowers of the Forest" and "Reveille."

OUR GREATEST BOXER
MICKEY MACINTYRE

*R*ing Magazine, the Bible of Boxing, nicknamed him "The Pride of Cape Breton." Mickey MacIntyre, a native of Dominion No. 4, flashed across boxing's firmament like a meteor.

The few existing accounts of his all-too-brief ring career cite him as Cape Breton's most outstanding boxer ever.

Halifax broadcaster and sportswriter Pat Connolly calls him "the greatest Cape Bretoner of all."

His citation in the Nova Scotia Sport Hall of Fame reads: "The 'Pride of Cape Breton' was the greatest boxer ever produced in the area."

Mickey was a classy boxer and a hard-hitting middleweight. When he died on October 2, 1922, the *Post-Record* headlined: "Fought Hundreds of Bouts in His Prime."

His best-known fight was in Winnipeg on July 12, 1912. His opponent in a twelve-round exhibition match was "Battling"

Fig. 18. Mickey MacIntyre "had it all," but the Cape Breton boxer disliked training. He also burned the candle at both ends (and "in the middle, too") and died at age 32. Fight historians rate him as the finest boxer ever to come out of Nova Scotia. Photographer unknown. Courtesy Gary Gallivan, Whitney Pier Museum.

Nelson, who had just lost his world lightweight title to Ad Wolgast. It was billed as a "no decision" bout, but ringsiders and sportswriters declared MacIntyre the winner.

An anonymous sportswriter from the *Victoria Daily Colonist* wrote: "MacIntyre had the advantage as Nelson was bleeding freely from the mouth, his left eye was closed while his right lamp was badly discoloured."

His boxing career began at age 17, when he entered and won the lightweight division of a tournament in Boston. Mickey was managed and trained by his brother-in-law Tom Casey, who was better known as Nova Scotia's Deputy Minister of Mines.

Pat Connolly wrote that "'Big Cy' MacDonald claimed a role as a travelling trainer, but methinks he was more of a camp follower when he was able to hitch a lift via CNR freights to the far stretches of the land, like 'Saskabush', for Mickey's fights and spun great stories to entertain the troops at Senator's Corner."

It must have been a thankless task for Tom Casey. Mickey hated to train and loved to party.

Mickey also had a brother, John Alex MacIntyre, a lesser boxer who settled in Detroit and became one of the best-known managers in the business. He brought several of his world-class fighters to Glace Bay for Gussie MacLellan's promotions in the 1940s. One member of his stable,

Lee Oma, fought "Tiger" Warrington and "Young Kid" McCoy, an outstanding welterweight.

Mickey came home from Boston and turned professional. His first opponent was hard-hitting Bernard "Kid" O'Neill. Mickey knocked him out in the second round.

He took on all comers as he barnstormed the Maritimes, western Canada and the United States. Some of his opponents were former world champions and some were welterweight crown contenders.

Halifax sportswriter "Gee" Ahern reported that Mickey lost a 1909 decision to "Billy Parsons, the sensational puncher from North Sydney. However, Mickey got his revenge and stopped Billy in seven rounds on March 7 and in thirteen on May 24."

In 1911, he didn't lose a bout and won the Canadian welterweight title.

Two years later, he gained worldwide attention when he defeated Billy Griffiths in Calgary.

In 1914, Mickey was only 24 and at his peak. He had just whipped the All-Ireland welterweight champion. But he had decided before a fight with Scottish champion Johnny Connolly that it would be his last fight. Connolly threw in the towel in the eighth round.

Mickey's supporters urged him to make a comeback. He came back for one last fight and battled championship contender Joe Rivers to a draw.

Mickey MacIntyre might have been a contender for the world championship had he not been reluctant to train.

He was generous to a fault; he gave his purses away to almost anyone who asked him for money. Out of the ring, he burned the candle at both ends. He lived the high life and was a hard drinker.

His candle guttered out at both ends in 1922 in a Sydney hospital. He was admitted to hospital, critically ill, on Sunday, 1 October. He died of pneumonia at 2 p.m. the following day. He was only 32.

MICKEY MacIntyre is an original member of the Nova Scotia Sport Hall of Fame.

AN ARTIST ON AND OFF THE ICE

"LILY" MACLELLAN

The late Jackie "Lily" MacLellan (He had a sister, Lily. The boyhood nickname stuck) was an artist on the ice – one of the highest scorers in Maritimes college and senior hockey.

Recently, seventeen of his oil paintings were donated by his family and will hang permanently in the Cape Breton Miners' Museum. He took up painting late in life and never had a formal lesson. He was never down in a coal mine. He saw mining through the eyes of his miner father.

When I saw the paintings my first impression was of Dante's inferno – hell underground in one of the most dangerous jobs in the world.

Montreal artist, Patricia Bourque, says: "I think the ones inside the mine are very powerful. I think he conveyed the claustrophobic feel, darkness and intensity of mining passionately.

"It's a unique collection. How often do you see paintings of inside a coal mine?"

Ottawa artist and electronic journalist, Pierre Bourque terms the collection "sober works of passion that clearly tell a unique story about mining life. I doubt any of these works would leave anyone cold!"

Unveiling the collection, Senator Frank Mahovlich said: "From the beautiful colours to details, such as mice in the mine and the family dealing with the explosion, Jack MacLellan has captured mining through painting.

"It tells the whole story of mining here in Glace Bay. I can appreciate it as my father was a gold miner for 25 years in Timmins, Ontario."

Dr. John Young, a 1955 St. FX University commerce graduate, now a Toronto artist and businessman, "discovered" MacLellan's work and encouraged him to make it public.

"He wouldn't hear of it."

"Jack only had one light, the light from the coal miner's helmet; the rest of the scene was as dark as it should be.

"The ability to capture reflected light is difficult for many artists. When I saw these paintings, I knew I was seeing genius."

After Jack died in 2002, John Young contacted his family. They agreed to donate the paintings to hang in the museum.

The museum – both underground and above – is a world-class exhibit. It is currently involved in an $8.5 million expansion fundraising campaign.

John Young cut a personal cheque to have the paintings framed and lit by a professional set designer. The paintings are hung along a passageway down the mine slope.

MACLELLAN was one of Nova Scotia's finest natural athletes.

He began his hockey career in Glace Bay with St. John's CYO. He centered a line with the Swartzack brothers, Eugene and Eddie (page 81).

The trio enrolled at St. FX University and their line remained intact. Together, they shredded college and senior record books. Speedy and gritty Warren Allmand was a team member.

They led St. FX to its sixth and seventh collegiate championships. It was a rare game if they did not score in double digits.

In a two-game, total-goals final, they outscored Mount Allison 17-1.

The line recorded 135 goals and 238 assists in 1950-51. Eddie Swartzack, not yet 18, scored 60 goals and assisted on 47, in 47 games.

Many, including Montreal sportswriter Andy O'Brien, felt that St. FX should represent Canada in the 1952 Oslo Olympics, saying: "They are so amateur that they buy their own skates and equipment."

The Olympic honour went to Edmonton Mercurys.

The X-Men won the prestigious invitational Renssaeler Polytechnic Institute tournament, Troy, New York, by knocking off host RPI, Brown and Princeton.

RPI coach Ned Harkness came to their dressing room afterwards and offered full hockey scholarships to every man in the room. There was one hitch: RPI was an Engineering School.

The X-Men tied a barnstorming Chicago Blackhawks team in an exhibition game. Eugene Swartzack remembers that former Montreal Junior Canadien, Paul McManaman, turned defenceman Al Dewsbury inside out and made goaltender Al Rollins look like a rookie.

JACKIE MacLellan's college roommate, "Stump" MacDonald, was a team manager. Jackie was well over six feet tall, Stump was well under. Walking together, they could be mistaken for "Mutt" and "Jeff."

A victory over Laval University in a Quebec tournament was occasion for celebration at the Chateau Frontenac hotel. Stump was unaccustomed to strong grog and wound up embracing the porcelain mistress in a hotel bathroom. Up came everything and down went his partial dental plate.

Room Service thought they had heard everything until a slurred voice called down and asked for a plumber and a dentist.

Eddie Swartzack was once asked if Lily could have played in major junior leagues, Eddie replied:

"Absolutely! He had an incredible shift. He could take any defenceman and put him in the second row. But, Jack was more interested in academics."

Jack was also a gifted baseball player. He hit a long ball. He roamed centerfield like a restless cat and could throw a strike to home plate. His junior team, Glace Bay's No. 11 Antonians, won the Maritime title in 1952.

BOXING, BOWLING AND BILLIARDS

JOE SMITH

Glace Bay clothier Joe Smith's clever newspaper ads always identified him as "the guy with the World Boxing Record."

He did, indeed, establish a world boxing record in the ring in an amateur tournament at the Boston Garden in 1930.

Joe's opponent was Walter Roachville, Interstate Middleweight Champion.

Joe knocked Roachville down nine times in the first round – a record that will never be eclipsed because of today's "three knockdown and out" rule. Roachville was down twice in the second round, but he survived the early punishment and knocked Joe out.

Joe just missed another rendezvous with boxing immortality in a main bout in Glace Bay in 1932. He knocked out Jimmy MacDougall of Sydney Mines in 14 seconds of the first round.

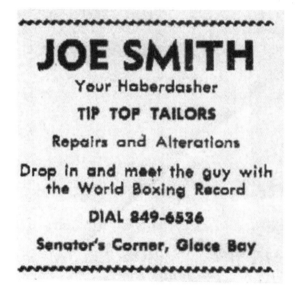

Fig. 19. Clipping from Post-Record, *date unknown. Courtesy Pat MacAdam.*

JOE Smith was born in Yorkshire, England on March 24, 1906. He was a baby in his mother's arms when his father emigrated to

Glace Bay "to work the coal." Joe had three sisters and three brothers.

The Smiths lived in the notorious "French block" on South Street across from the ballpark. The row of ten residences has been described as "the worst slum in Glace Bay."

Glace Bay fish merchant Raymond Goldman recalled that the South Street ballpark was surrounded by a high board fence.

"In the spring, there wouldn't be one board left. The French block people used the boards for firewood," he said.

Joe played intermediate rugby with the Caledonia team, but he was later disqualified as an amateur because he had boxed professionally.

He started boxing in 1924 when he was eighteen. In 1925, during the bitter miners' strike when William Davis was shot and killed, Joe left Glace Bay, like many others, to find work in "the Boston States."

After several years in Boston, he came home and found work in Caledonia colliery.

One of Joe's proudest boasts was that he was at the finish line in 1926 when the pride of Florence, 19 year-old upstart Johnny Miles, won his first Boston Marathon in world record time. Miles finished four minutes ahead of Olympic gold medal marathoner, Albin Stenroos of Finland.

While working in the pit, Joe won the Maritime middleweight championship.

For a time, Joe's trainer was "Chief Joe" MacInnis, chief of police in Glace Bay.

In the early 1920s, in a ten-round bout with Billy Holm, "The Fighting Dane" from New Waterford, in the Russell Theatre in Glace Bay, Joe lost by a technical knockout in the fourth round. He took one of the worst beatings of his young life.

On October 26, 1933, Joe exacted his revenge.

The *Post-Record* reported:

GLACE BAY—"Dynamite" Joe Smith, of Caledonia, battered Bill Holm, "The Fighting Dane" from New Waterford, all around the ring for eight of ten rounds tonight, but although Holm took a seven count, two eights and a nine and was practically out on his feet several times, he weathered the storm, taking one of the worst lickings a fighter ever received in a Glace Bay ring.

JOE'S boxing career took him across Canada and the United States. He was New England amateur light heavyweight champion. He had 64 amateur fights and won 57. He turned professional and won the Maritime light heavyweight title. He won 38 of 43 pro fights before he retired.

Joe was not a one-dimensional person. He was not a one-trick pony. He fashioned a full life when his ring career was over.

Reggie O'Neill of Sydney River grew up in Glace Bay and, as a teenager, worked for Joe as a clerk in Smith's Tip Top Tailors clothing store on Union Street, just off Senator's Corner. Joe's main competitor, Hugh MacIntyre's Society Brand store, was just a chip shot away.

Reggie remembers that Joe was not a tailor. He took measurements and they were sent off to Toronto. If alterations were needed, they were done by Gerd Bruckschwaigher in his tiny second-floor shop above Toby and Ein's, next door to Knox Hall. Gerd is still in the needle trade with a shop across the street from Mayflower Mall, on Grand Lake Road.

Joe was a shrewd businessman. His display ads in the *Post-Record* were a combination of satire, sports gossip, social commentary and subliminal marketing.

Senator John Buchanan recalls that Joe took delight in twitting him in his column for being the only member of the Buchanan family not born in Glace Bay.

"When I was premier, no visit to Glace Bay was complete without a pit-stop at Joe's tailor shop," Buchanan recalled.

Did Joe offer a belt of Lemon Gin and Lime Rickey?

"Yes, and I took it!" Buchanan said.

Joe also delighted in poking fun at the "homers" in the *Post-Record*'s sports department.

One of his *Post-Record* columns – sometimes called "Joe's Stuff" and sometimes called "Sez Joe" – asked readers: "Did you read in the *Post-Record* that Sydney Millionaires clobbered Glace Bay Miners 2-1 and two nights later the Miners edged Sydney 9-1?"

Joe's haberdashery catered to the young, dressy set. Hugh MacIntyre's clientele was older and more conservative.

Former Cape Breton County Councillor Donald MacIsaac remembers that the difference between a good year and a bad year was the contract for uniforms for police and firemen.

"Joe was lucky to get it one out of every four years. Hughie MacIntyre had a lock on it because most of the town councillors were customers of his. I think the profit on the uniform contract was $2,000.

"Joe didn't get rich running his clothing store. He netted $4,000-$5,000 in a good year."

One of Joe's merchandising gimmicks was his Suit Club. Members paid $1 a week and had a chance to win a free suit. If they didn't win, the $1 was still applied to the suit they were buying.

Not a year went by that Joe did not sponsor a softball team in a local industrial league or a Little League baseball team. He was a fair-to-middling softball pitcher himself.

Joe also donated an Adam hat to any Glace Bay Miner hockey player who scored a hat-trick. He had the benefit of exposure on the Forum's public address system and, after most games, the winner's name was mentioned in the *Post-Record* in the game account.

Reggie O'Neill remembers Joe as a thoughtful and generous employer.

"Joe was a real spiffy dresser, always dressed to the nines. He exuded charm and made everyone feel good. He was active in bridge, bowling, golf and billiards."

Donald MacIsaac remembers Joe as a scratch golfer at Lingan Golf and Country Club, but Joe's finest achievements were in bowling and billiards. He bowled with several championship teams and won Nova Scotia and Maritime billiards championships.

When Joe Smith and Joe Valentine chalked up over a game of billiards in Steve Markadonis's poolroom, activity at all other tables stopped and the players gathered to watch. Joe had "soft hands" and a gentle touch with his cue.

Donald MacIsaac says that Joe had a regulation size billiards table in his home on Brookside Street: "I did his books and when I dropped by his store, he'd say right off the bat: 'I ran 115 last night or I ran 100'."

Joe Smith is the man who started Ring 73 Veterans Boxing Association in Glace Bay—the first ever in Canada. Two years later it became an amateur boxing club.

Joe was inducted in the Canadian Boxing Hall of Fame on July 23, 1977. He passed away in Glace Bay on Christmas Day, 1997. He was 91.

COMBAT ZONE
HALLOWEEN IN GLACE BAY

When I was a kid growing up in Glace Bay in the 1940s, it took awhile for the town to recover from Halloween. The whole town looked like a combat zone the day after.

Dynamite and blasting caps were easy to come by in a coal mining town. A stick or two, a cap, a long wire and a flashlight battery could make an outhouse disappear. Small town kids weren't up on the basic laws of physics. They didn't know that a blast followed the path of least resistance. This was usually the clean-out door at the bottom of the biffy. Poor Donald John MacLean's two-holer was located too close to his house. For the next month or so, he could be seen hosing down the side of his house with a garden hose.

"Whiz-bangs" were other explosive devices that were available in quantity and easy to steal. They were little torpedoes that railway section hands placed on the track to warn locomotive engineers to slow down or stop.

When an engine ran over a "whiz-bang," it exploded with a loud crack. You could probably detonate one by hitting it with a sledgehammer – at your peril. They were really small hand grenades with the potential for serious bodily harm.

Bobbing for apples was too tame for some bad kids. Soaping car and house windows was kid stuff. They were out for big game. Nothing was sacred. They would tie a stout rope to a front fence near a bus stop, wait for the next bus to come by and then tie the other end of the rope to the bus bumper. Voila! Thirty feet of fencing skipped down the street behind the bus.

One of the more devious tricks was to pick up an outhouse and move it back six or eight feet. The unsuspecting homeowner, accustomed to pacing off the usual steps, didn't know what hit him until he dropped down four or five feet.

One of the standard Halloween games was playing "purse" – just like that amusing TV commercial with the grizzly bear and the turtle. A lady's handbag or purse or a man's wallet would be dropped on the sidewalk with a string attached.

A passerby, hopefully a little old lady, would walk by in the dark and see the "purse" on the sidewalk. Just as her fingers touched it, kids hiding in the bushes would yank the string. There were no known coronaries. They made little old ladies tough in mining towns, too.

ONE Halloween my brother Austin and our first cousin Stevie put sheets over themselves and hid behind gravestones at an abandoned cemetery on King Edward Street. Blair Vacheresse came lurching home after a hard night at a booze can on Lower Main Street.

Austin and Stevie jumped out at him and Blair's hair stood on end. He took to his heels. The guys had a great laugh and waited for their next victim. Suddenly, there was the unmistakable crack of a Cooey .22 rifle. Lead slugs were pinging off the grave stones. Blair was ghost busting from his upstairs bedroom window.

Austin and Stevie were pinned down behind stones until Blair ran out of ammunition.

Every home in Glace Bay had a clothesline in the back yard. Unless it was illuminated by a strong spotlight, it was toast. It didn't do just to cut the line. A foot-long section had to be removed from the middle so it couldn't be spliced.

My cousin Stevie was a serial clothesline cutter. It all began the night he was fleeing some irate homeowner on his bicycle. Stevie took a short cut through P. J. Cadegan's back yard and got "clothes-lined." The line caught him on the Adam's apple and knocked him off his bike. After that, he never saw a clothesline he liked.

Letting the air out of car tires was child's play. The more creative (and energetic) kids would lift a Volkswagen Beetle and place it sideways in the entrance to a downtown store or in the back of a pick-up truck.

The town police were powerless to act. All the tires on their squad cars and motorcycles were flat. The three-man RCMP detachment turned a blind eye. Their job was busting up stills and apprehending moonshiners. They were prepared to go up against clubs and shotguns, but they wouldn't take on crazy Glace Bay kids.

The windows in the principal's office at St. Anne's high school were routinely "pucked out" with stones and crab apples. The principal, a Halifax Sister of Charity, was probably the most unpopular teacher in town. When she administered the thick leather strap to the palms of your hands, it was done in her office with the public address system turned up full blast.

One day, she drew the strap up and over her shoulder and was preparing to come down on Paddy O'Donnell's hand. At the last second, Paddy pulled his hand back and she hit herself on the thigh. Her scream of pain was heard over the PA system in every classroom.

Some parents believed the only way to mitigate the damage on Halloween was to organize driveway parties with apple bobbing in giant washtubs, co-op fireworks displays and ghost-story telling sessions. After listening to the Scottish stories of the *bocains* (spooks), we all looked under our beds when we said our prayers.

Then, along came an initiative that saved the town from total destruction. The nuns passed out UNICEF boxes and we went door to door collecting for the under-privileged kids of the world.

On Sunday mornings, the parish priest, Father M. A. MacAdam, thundered from his pulpit against the miscreants who had inflicted damage. He was particularly incensed when someone removed a large plaster statue of the Blessed Virgin from his altar and stuck her on the lawn of the Canadian Legion building.

The Mother of Christ had a quart beer bottle taped to her outstretched palm. On her head was a Legion beret. It wasn't entirely sacrilegious. The beret had a Cape Breton Highlanders cap badge.

The statue was not damaged and was returned to St. Anne's church.

In World War II, the Germans called the kilted Cape Breton Highlanders (the "C. B. *haitch*") "the ladies from hell." The regiment had a reputation as a collection of fierce warriors. Little did the Germans realize that most of them were advanced explosives experts long before they joined the army.

BORN TO SPEED

Is the urge to speed in your genes? Are some people born to speed? My romance with speed began when I saw movie newsreels of my hero, fighter ace "Buzz" Beurling's Spitfire war.

I was a juvenile Walter Mitty. I daydreamed I was a Spitfire pilot. I wanted to be "Buzz" Beurling. I kept a scrapbook about him. After the war, I saw him fly his personal Tiger Moth in a Sydney air show.

For only $5, "Buzz" would take you up for a flip. But what kid had $5? My Da was working as a coal company machinist for what was likely less than $5 a day.

At summer camp we had an annual sports day – sprints, relays and potato sack races. The winners won wartime nut bars named after Liberator and Beaufort bombers. Sugar and chocolate were rationed. The nut bars tasted awful.

My specialties were the 100 and 220-yard dashes. I won the 100 and an hour or so later lined up for the 220 – to the flagpole and back. I won that too. Father "Hank" Nash beckoned me over and told me if I had grabbed the pole and swung myself around instead of running wide I would have broken the Nova Scotia schoolboy record for the 220.

However, my blinding speed served me well dodging coal company cops, Sydney & Louisburg Railway "bulls" and town police trying to catch me raiding local gardens.

My pride and joy was my heavy wooden luge sled. It was built clandestinely in the coal company's Big Shops. My uncle, Frank Gallivan, forged the runners in the blacksmith's shop.

My Da smuggled it out, piece by piece, and assembled and painted it at home. I called her "Red Racer."

"Red Racer" and I bonded. We were as one. I talked to her, urging her to go even faster down steep Lower King Edward

Street. I started my run on the red rocket at the corner of King Edward and Main alongside the house where the late, great CBC reporter Bill MacNeil was born. One day I passed a car being driven slowly by an old codger. I passed under it from rear to front. The old guy must have almost suffered a coronary when he saw a sled shoot out in front of his hood.

Thank God "Red Racer" was low slung!

The town police paid "Red Racer" and me the ultimate compliment. Chief Joe MacInnis himself came out to collar us, but his prowl car couldn't possibly match my speed on the icy street.

To compound his frustration, he didn't know who I was. I had a woollen scarf wrapped around my lower face to fend off cinders and horse pucks. I can conjure up a phantasm of the Chief going back to the station and telling his men: "Missed him again! Just who is that masked man anyway?"

Rosebud, eat your heart out!

TWO of my first cousins were also obsessed with speed, but they were a couple of sandwiches short of a picnic. One of them liked to ride his bicycle on the main highway between Glace Bay and Sydney. He'd aim his bike at an oncoming bus and play a game of chicken. Lucky for him, the bus driver always chickened out first.

My other cousin wasn't as lucky. He drove his 1940s DeSoto coupe like an Indy 500 racecar driver. The "Judique Flyer" passenger train ran once a week between the Strait of Canso and Inverness. My cousin tried to outrun it at a level crossing, he managed to hit it and live.

Could it just possibly be my cousins and I were the original "Crazy Canucks" – a quarter of a century before skiers Ken Read, Dave Murray, Dave Irwin, Jim Hunter and Steve Podborski?

Skis were scarcer than hen's teeth in industrial Cape Breton, because there were no slopes anywhere except in the Highlands, 100 miles away.

Nevertheless, I crafted a pair of skis from two staves of a molasses puncheon. I sanded the staves until they were glassy smooth and then waxed them with Johnson's Shinola paste wax until they gleamed. Then I tacked on leather bootstraps, kitted myself out with broom handles for poles and went off to the *piste*.

The *piste* was Jimmy MacKay's "Fox Farm," a large tract of scrubland covered with pimples that wouldn't qualify as moguls at Camp Fortune. The "Fox Farm" was also scarred with the remains of bootleg coal pits eight to ten feet deep.

The moment of truth had arrived. I found the highest point of land and pushed off. What a rush! I was skiing. I poled furiously to go even faster and then fell off the end of the earth, when the snow crust over a bootleg pit broke and I dropped in it. I thought I had broken every bone in my body. Beam me up, Scotty! I never attempted to ski again.

The only equal pain I experienced was when I was playing cops and robbers running through a darkened, abandoned service station – firing my cap pistol over my shoulder.

"Bang, bang, I got you. You're dead."

Except it wasn't my pursuer who almost got dead. It was me. I ran full tilt into the grease pit, hit the far wall and crumbled in a heap at the bottom. I wasn't worried about being killed or maimed. I was more worried about going home to face my Ma and Da, bruised and bloodied, my clothes all ripped and covered in grease from stem to gudgeon.

My dazzling speed was then relegated to thousands of hours of shinny on frozen ponds, bogs, marshes and rivers. On weekends we played hockey from dawn to dusk. We prayed we wouldn't "fall in" and come out looking like human Popsicles, because it was a long walk home a mile away.

We weren't pampered like today's kids. We walked everywhere, kitbags slung over our shoulders. A 6 a.m. practice in the Glace Bay Miners' Forum, a mile away, could only possibly be equalled by ice time in Maple Leaf Gardens.

Skates were hand-me-downs. A hockey stick had to last an entire winter and the blade was a toothpick by spring. Eaton's and Simpson's catalogues were our shin pads and, if we couldn't afford a puck, we used a road apple or a shoe polish can.

The cops often broke up street hockey games, but they operated under a handicap. They weren't on skates.

Years later I flew *Concorde* to Heathrow. We flew Mach 2, 1,360 mph at 57,500 feet. I was disappointed. It didn't seem as if we were flying twice the speed of sound, not like the times I went screaming down Lower King Edward Street.

Now that was speed.

STAINED GLASS

Through the violence and hatred found in the clash of cultures, ideologies and religions, there is at least one small oasis of sanity where brotherhood and love are alive and well.

They live in peace in a small United Church in Inverness.

DURING World War II, eight of Inverness's non-Catholic young men lost their lives. A personalized stained glass window in St. Matthew's United Church remembers each one. Three of the large windows honour Jewish servicemen who died on active service.

Lieutenant Jack Levine was killed on his 21st birthday on July 2, 1944, near Caen, France. His final resting place is a British military cemetery in Hottot-les-Bagues, France. The focal point of his stained glass window is a Star of David.

Two of Isador and Fanny Feinstein's four sons went off to war, never to return.

Flight Sergeant Sam Feinstein went directly into the Royal Canadian Air Force from high school. He was killed on September 30, 1942, a tail gunner in a Twelve Squadron Wellington bomber that was shot down over enemy territory.

Sam is buried in a Commonwealth War Grave in Bergen, Holland. His window in St. Matthew's is centred by a burning bush.

Nathan Feinstein was a 27 year-old private with the North Nova Scotia Highlanders. He was killed in action on the southern shore of the Scheldt estuary in the fierce battle at the Leopold Canal crossing.

He is buried in Adegem Canadian War Cemetery midway between Brugge and Ghent. His memorial window features a dove with an olive branch.

The inscription above windows is a quotation from Ecclesiasticus: "Their Name Liveth for Evermore."

Under the windows is the inscription: "Dedicated to the glory of God in honour of those who served and in memory of those who made the Supreme Sacrifice in World War II 1939-45 by St. Matthew's congregation."

The windows were dedicated shortly after the war ended and were paid for by "congregational subscription."

Congregational subscription was no small financial matter. St. Matthew's Church is a mission church among four small St. John's Pastoral Charge churches. Located in Inverness's county seat, it has only 130 families in its flock.

The village of Inverness, with a total population of 1,935, is predominantly Roman Catholic. It is one of Cape Breton's major centres of Scottish culture – fiddling, piping, step dancing and folk music.

United Church Minister Reverend Donald B. Willmer says: "The population of Inverness County is, as you might guess, almost entirely of the Christian faith and the majority of people, being of Highland Scot descent, adhere to the Roman Catholic denomination. There are only two church buildings in Inverness, so the United Church is sort of the 'residual' denomination."

In this mix of Catholics and Protestants, there were only two Hebrew families in all of Inverness – the Levines and the Feinsteins.

MORRIS Levine was born in Montreal where he met Lena, his bride-to-be. When they met he was attempting to organize T. Eaton Company workers. He was forced to move to New York when no Canadian employer would hire him because of his union activities.

Morris's father-in-law owned and operated Wener's dry goods store in Inverness. When he died, Morris continued to operate Wener and Levine.

Inverness was a boomtown in the early 1900s. Once a small community dependent solely on the fishery, it mushroomed when bituminous coal was found and a major underground mine was opened. Inverness coal was shipped to Prince Edward Island, Maine and Europe. The village prospered to the extent that the mine owners built eighty houses for their workers.

The Levines were popular members of the community. Reverend Willmer says: "We are told that Morris taught classes in ballroom dancing, at the request of the Catholic Women's League!"

The Levines had two sons, Jack and Art, and four daughters. Jack's early life was full with promise. At Acadia University he was editor of the college newspaper and captain of the debating team. He intended to go to medical school.

When he graduated in 1943 he attended officers' training school and was commissioned a second lieutenant. Following further training at Aldershot, Nova Scotia, he was commissioned a full lieutenant.

He answered a call from the British Army for platoon leaders and served with the Second Gloucestershire Regiment until he was killed in action.

His brother Art still lives in Inverness with his wife Anita – a block away from St. Matthew's Church. They are the only Jews in Inverness.

Isador and Fanny Feinstein lived in Inverness until Isador's death in the early 1940s. Fanny moved to Toronto. The Feinstein's four sons were first cousins to Jack and Art Levine.

Fanny Feinstein and Lena Levine were part of a circle of women friends from St. Matthew's congregation. They attended United Church women's meetings and played cards with the women of the church.

SAXBY Blair is the only one of the eight non-Catholics who "is home" – buried in St. Matthew's churchyard. He was an RCAF Leading Air Craftsman who was killed at age 23 in Yorkton, Saskatchewan, on June 16, 1941, during night flying training in a Harvard.

Donald Ross was a 26 year-old merchant mariner who was on board the Canadian National Steamships' SS *Lady Hawkins* when she was torpedoed by *U-66* off North Carolina on January 19, 1942. There were only 71 survivors of 321 passengers and crew.

Gunner Joe Varrence, 22, Royal Canadian Artillery, died on active service in Newfoundland, February 24, 1944. He is buried in Mount Pleasant Cemetery, St. John's.

Jack Watson, 34, Winnipeg Grenadiers, was killed in action on December 21, 1942. He is buried in Brookside Cemetery, Winnipeg.

Rifleman Fred Wyras, 24, Royal Rifles of Canada, is buried in a war cemetery in Yokohama, Japan. He was taken prisoner when Hong Kong fell to the Japanese and he died on Christmas Eve 1944, in captivity as a forced labourer in Japan.

MORRIS and Lena Levine are buried in Glace Bay. Isador and Fanny Feinstein are buried in Toronto. Their two younger sons, Bernard and John, emigrated to Israel and died there.

Art Levine sticks close to Inverness. He has never been to France to visit his brother's grave.

REMEMBERING THE *POST RECORD*

The wages of a coal company machinist in Glace Bay's "Big Shops" couldn't be stretched to subsidize two sons at St. FX. So, between graduation from St. Anne's in 1951 and enrolment at St. FX in 1952, I spent fifteen heady months as a news and sports reporter with the *Post Record* in Glace Bay. In high school, I was the *Post's* stringer and phoned in results of St. Anne's rugby, hockey and basketball games to Herbie Stevens.

When Herbie left the *Post Record* for bigger and better things with Canadian Press in the Big Smoke, Joe Hines called me and offered me his job. I was sixteen going on seventeen. He asked me if I could type. I couldn't, but lied. Days later, when I saw Ted Boutilier bashing a standard Underwood with two fingers, I knew mastering typing wouldn't be difficult.

The starting pay was $20 a week and a free paper.

My first assignment might have been my last, if I hadn't had an understanding boss in Joe Hines. He sent me out to cover a meeting of organizers for Glace Bay's 50th anniversary. The chairman listed all the service clubs, churches and volunteer groups who were playing key roles.

One of the groups was Hadassah. Growing up on Catholic Chapel Hill, I had never heard of Hadassah and didn't know how to spell it. I made a mental note to ask someone after the meeting, but forgot. So Hadassah was not mentioned in the story in the paper the next day.

The Jewish community was incensed and let Joe Hines know it in no uncertain terms. He was deluged with phone calls, many of them from prominent Jewish merchants who were major advertisers. Joe managed to calm them down before the error of omission reached the ears of *Post Record* publisher Roy Duchemin in Sydney.

115

Joe didn't have to offer up my head, but I am convinced the Sydney owners would have sacked me had they known.

The next fifteen months were exciting ones for a teenage kid whose heroes were Shaun MacDonald, Gene Fowler, "Red" Smith, "Speed" Galley, Ann Terry MacLellan, Gussie MacLellan, Aubrey Keizer and Nathan Cohen.

Nathan started his career at the *Glace Bay Gazette* and hardly a week passed that the fire department wasn't called to the *Gazette's* second floor office on Senator's Corner. Absent minded Nathan had the bad habit of flipping lit cigarette butts into waste baskets.

Big time hockey came to Glace Bay in 1951 thanks to a citizens' group headed up by shoe repair shop owner John Xidos. Former Toronto Maple Leaf "Bud" Poile was signed as playing coach. He was flanked on the first line by future NHLers Len "Comet" Haley and Jimmy Anderson.

Sheldon Bloomer was lured away from the Providence Reds. Elliott "Specs" Chorley had won the Western Junior scoring championship the previous season. Hub Macey played thirty NHL games over three seasons with New York Rangers and Montreal Canadiens and came to the Bay from Tulsa.

Cliff Hicks was a cool, stand-up goaltender who had enjoyed outstanding seasons with Ontario's junior Guelph Biltmore Madhatters and Chicoutimi Sagueneens of the powerful Quebec Senior League.

It was Triple-A hockey on a par with the American Hockey League and just a notch below the NHL. The Miners or any of the six teams in the league would give any of today's NHL teams a run for their money.

The Miners' opening games were away games and the *Post Record* decided I should travel with the team to Moncton and Charlottetown on the team bus leased from Acadian Lines. I was given a $20 travel advance for two hotel nights and came home with change. A room in the Queen's Hotel in downtown Moncton was $2 a night.

On the way home our bus skidded on an icy road at Loch Broom, Pictou County, and ended up on its side in the ditch. The only slight injury was to Bud Poile's leg when my heavy portable typewriter flew out of the overhead bin and hit him.

MY SHIFT started at 7 p.m., so I had all day to hone my snooker skills in the Casino Billiard Academy against Bud Poile, Hub Macey, Ron Rohmer, Johnny Myketyn, Cliff Hicks and local sharks like Albert Poole, Wilsie MacIntyre, Edgar Connors, Donald MacIsaac, Hazen MacDonald and Jackie Hines.

Most weeks I made double the money the paper paid me by shooting pool. Bud Poile was the toughest player to beat.

He played a wicked, low key, slow paced, psychological game.

My first career came to an end in September, 1952. By then I was earning $40 a week. I accompanied the Junior No. 11 Antonians' baseball team to Springhill to play the Fence Busters for the provincial championship. Springhill won a closely fought series. Returning home, the team bus stopped in front of Mockler Hall at St. FX and let me off. I was three days late registering and none too kindly received by the Registrar.

I hoped to go "home" to join in Glace Bay's 100th-anniversary celebrations and the Sons of Israel's 100th – Kum-A-Haym. I looked forward to swapping lies with Clarence Sampson, Donald MacInnis, Gus O'Neill and looking up "Digger" MacKenzie at his retirement home at Big Glace Bay Lake. Perhaps I'd share a laugh with Archie Shore or Raymond Goldman over my Hadassah gaffe 50 years earlier.

But it was not to be. Fate intervened. My only brother, Austin, an African missionary priest, died from brain cancer in Washington. His order, the White Fathers of Africa, offered to bury him in a plot they owned in Gate of Heaven Cemetery in the U.S. capitol. I declined with thanks.

I told them I would take him home to Glace Bay and bury him with our parents.

In 43 years in the priesthood, Austin had many bivouacs: Antigonish; Alexandria Bay, New York; Eastview, Ontario; Rome; Masaka and Kampala, Uganda; the Black townships, South Africa; Jesuit universities in Dayton, Ohio, and St. Louis, Missouri; and his last postings in Chicago and Washington.

Many bivouacs, but only one barracks ever, and that was Glace Bay. When he was in North America he never missed coming home every summer for three weeks to relieve at St. Anne's while the regular clergy took their holidays.

Austin maintained an account at the Glace Bay Central Credit Union for more than fifty years and he came to know "Big Cy" MacDonald well. Big Cy and his wife were the custodians of the Credit Union and lived above the store. Austin never tired of hearing Big Cy tell and re-tell his outrageous tales.

Austin was a Canon lawyer and earned his doctorate at the Gregorian College, Rome, and in Dayton and St. Louis. He could debate Friedrich Nietzsche, Soren Kierkegaard, Thomas Aquinas, Karl Marx, Friedrich Engels and Chairman Mao but the philosopher he doted on most was Big Cy.

"GOOD FOR US TO BE HERE"

THE CLERGY IN CAPE BRETON

I stayed up late one night to watch the movie *Going My Way*. It suddenly occurred to me that when I was a young boy in Glace Bay, Father "Hank" Nash was Bing Crosbie to Father M. A. MacAdam's Barry Fitzgerald.

Our parents had no need to fear the parish priests or curates who shaped our characters. Men like Father "Hank" Nash, Father "Butch" MacLean and Father "Shorty" Roussell were he-men. The only body contact between us was the odd elbow or butt-end of a hockey stick when we played hockey with them on a frozen pond or river.

St. Anne's parish was the hub of our lives. Curates like Father Nash were the dynamic catalysts who enhanced our quality of life. He was an organizer, a motivator, a fundraiser, a scrounger and sometimes a basketball and hockey coach. Father M. A. was a builder and a shrewd money manager, but he was in the autumn of life.

Father Nash had a dream of a summer camp for the kids of the parish and he made it happen at George's River. The men of the parish gave up their spare hours and weekends to build a chapel, cookhouse, outhouses and wooden platforms for a couple of dozen huge bell and wall tents.

The camp motto was: *Domine nos est hic bonum esse* (Lord it is good for us to be here).

Every kid in the parish was guaranteed two weeks on the shores of the Bras D'Or Lake whether or not his or her family could pay the small $10 fee.

Father Nash's camp was as close to Utopia or Brigadoon as a kid could get. I was Huck Finn, Holden Caulfield and James Dean rolled up in one happy camper. Camp was a happy cross between Boot Camp and Club Med. Us kids were happier than a dog with two tails.

We slept the sleep of the innocent under canvas. In the morning, we washed, brushed our teeth and combed our hair in a trickle of a stream and went off to Mass before breakfast.

Then came tent inspection, and Father Nash did not brook sloppiness. Untidy tents meant demerits and KP, picking up trash or whitewashing stones.

The days were carefree and fun-filled with softball, ping pong, badminton, foot races and bracing swims in the cold salt water of an inland sea – the Bras D'Or Lake. A rite of passage was a quarter-mile swim out to Mouse Island and back.

A race to Mouse Island was no contest if you were swimming against Dannie Bedecki. He was born with webs between his toes and he swam like an otter.

Another rite of passage was the annual day-long hike. Lunchtime baloney sandwiches never tasted so good.

Once a summer, someone "got the paddle." He committed an unforgivable act that warranted extreme corporal punishment. The miscreant was made to stand, touching his toes, and Father Nash delivered a whack on his backside with a small canoe paddle. The whole camp formed a circle and watched. Then, the disgraced camper was sent home to perhaps an even more severe paddling from his parents.

CAMP food stuck to your ribs and was plentiful. At lunch and supper, every kid was allotted two slices of bread. So, the boarding house reach prevailed as everyone grabbed for his two slices.

One camper, Alex MacKinnon, was always first among equals. He would yell: "I want my two slices." His nickname became "Two Slices" MacKinnon and remained with him through life – even when he became Father "Two Slices" MacKinnon of the Scarborough Foreign Missions.

A Roman collar did not provide dispensation from a nickname. Father Malcolm MacEachern, later Bishop of Charlottetown, stood six foot six. He was known as "Long Mal" or the "High Priest."

There was Father "Shorty, who was well over six feet tall, and Father "Butch," who was as thin as a rake. Father Alex started in life as an apprentice in a print shop – printer's "devil." He went through life as "Alex the Devil."

When Father Hughie was ordained a priest and became a choirmaster, he was known as "Tantum Ergo Hughie."

"Angus the Priest" MacGillivray wasn't a priest. He earned his nickname because he was a handyman for the Bishop. Another Angus MacGillivray went by the nickname of "Angus the Nun," because he was custodian at a convent. A bishop of Antigonish who shifted priests frequently was known (behind his back) as "Willie the Mover."

Father M. A. MacAdam was a stern disciplinarian. Parishioners joked that he smiled once, but that it wasn't really a smile. It was indigestion from a rogue cucumber.

The only known occasion when Father M. A.'s humour shone through was during one Sunday High Mass. A local doctor's wife liked to arrive fashionably late, make a grand entrance and sashay down the centre aisle to a front seat. She always wore a new hat or a new frock.

One Sunday, Father M. A. had had enough. The dowager arrived just as he was starting his sermon. She was halfway down the aisle when he halted in mid-sentence and said to the congregation: "I will wait until the Queen Mary docks."

She was never late again.

ANOTHER story, perhaps apocryphal, is of one of Father Nash's athletic protégés who was home for a holiday. She had been an outstanding gymnast in high school and had made it big with a U.S. circus.

The church was empty, so Father Nash asked her to perform a few flips and cartwheels in the aisle near the confessional box. Just at that precise moment, two little old ladies entered the church. One turned to the other and said: "My God, look what Father M. A. is giving for penance, and me with patched bloomers."

Perhaps one of the most outrageous stories to come out of St. Anne's was about a coal company machinist. He worked in the "big shops" servicing and maintaining locomotives and underground mining equipment.

Anything not nailed down at the end of a shift was toast. Steel rails weighing a ton and a half sometimes vanished. I have often wondered why anyone would want to steal a rail.

Our good thief plodded his way home up Chapel Hill burdened down with pilfered property. Nevertheless, when he passed by the front of St. Anne's church, he put his load down, blessed himself, loaded up again and proceeded on home.

He stole so much his wife became worried. Their basement and outside shed were full of useless items – things they couldn't possibly use. She was beginning to believe he was a kleptomaniac.

Since there was no psychiatrist in town, she made an appointment to see the parish priest. The pastor listened to her attentively and then asked her husband: "John Angus, have you ever made a Novena?"

John Angus replied: "No, Father, but if you have the plans, I have the nails and the lumber."

CAPE BRETON NICKNAMES

Charles de Gaulle looked down his ample patrician nose at his fellow countrymen and pronounced the French Republic ungovernable. In what must have been a moment of utter pique and sheer frustration, he exclaimed: "How can one govern a country that has 350 kinds of cheese?"

What might he have said had he been a local politician in industrial Cape Breton? Someone once described eastern Nova Scotia as: "Rainy days, Holy Days and MacDonalds."

At one time, DOSCO, the coal and steel company, had 650 MacDonalds on the payroll and 150 of them were named John.

One day, a car left Glace Bay headed for Sydney with five John MacDonalds in it – Jack "Spud," Johnny "Angus Summer John," Johnny "Flat," Johnny "Billy Big Archie" and Johnny "Billy Allan Cape North." Behind them, in a second car, were two more John MacDonalds – Jack "The Snake" and "Antigonish Jack."

Nicknames were the only means of singling out the many MacDonald families.

THE late Tony Mackenzie lived in Egerton, near Merigomish in Pictou County. He was a retired history teacher who collected and published Scots folklore. He attended St. Francis Xavier University off-and-on and left to work on hydro lines and in construction when funds ran out. He earned an arts degree in 1947 and 12 years later an education degree.

He joked that he attended university for three terms – "Roosevelt, Truman and Eisenhower."

Tony has two modest best-sellers on Maritime bookstore shelves and a third recently released. His history, *The Harvest Train*, is about Maritimers who rode the rails to western Canada for the grain harvest. His second book is titled *The Irish in Cape Breton*. His third chronicles visits of Gypsies to Atlantic Canada.

He also collected nicknames.

His favourite was the "Pickle Arse" Petries. The story goes that a Petrie was sitting on a barrel of pickled herring, fell into a political argument and then into the barrel of brine when the wooden cover caved in. He was wedged there firmly for some time, and when he was finally extricated, his posterior was pickled.

The "Pickle Arse" Petries are not to be confused with the "Proud Arse" MacLeans, who were the very first family in Iona to build an outdoor privy.

MOST nicknames reflect an ancestor, a physical characteristic, place of birth, a deformity or a misfortune.

Johnny "The Nun" worked at a convent. Billy "Concrete" had a son nicknamed Carl "Reddi-Mix." "Jim the Bear" had a son named "Colin the Cub." "Waterloo Dan" was a miner who had been branded in his youth. When he stripped in the colliery washhouse, there, printed backwards across his cheeks, was "Waterloo No. 2," a campaign ribbon he won when he backed into a red-hot stove.

History does not record how "Rotten Archie" came by his nickname. It could be from the Gaelic word *rotan*, which means red-faced. "Hughie the Crock" could have been a boozer, or his nickname could be from *cnoc*, the Gaelic word for hill pronounced "crok."

One can only wonder how "Big Angus the Clap" got his name. To give him the benefit of the doubt, the Gaelic word *clab* means garrulous.

Then there are the "Split the Winds." Their nickname was earned when the matriarch, without intending to, uncorked a blast of stomach gases that shook the stained glass windows and loosened the Stations of the Cross from the walls of St. Anne's Church in Glace Bay.

Tony MacKenzie's eyes gleamed when he related the story of "Five Mile Annie," who was married to "Two Storey Dan." She got her nickname because she drove her old car so slowly, and he got his because he was so tall he didn't need a ladder to paint the side of a house.

One day, "Two Storey Dan" had to resort to using a ladder and fell off. When Annie heard the news her only question was: "Did he spill any paint?"

There are no footnotes anywhere to tell how the "Blue" Macdonalds earned their nickname – unless it was for their Tory upbringing.

Angus "Blue" was a much-loved local politician in Glace Bay. He parlayed his job as a miner and his volunteer work with the Canadian Legion and Little League Baseball into a lifetime position on town council.

Like so many of his peers, Angus Blue left school at an early age to help support his family. His formal education probably ended with Grade 6. Blue was known for his propensity to mangle the English language. He could, on occasion, make Mrs. Malaprop sound like an Oxford don.

Addressing voters, he referred to them as "my dear constitionaries." If elected, he promised he would "do something about the 'Lightning' system on South Street." During a town council meeting, he advised those present he had difficulty pronouncing clerk Enso Antonello's name and thereafter would refer to him as "the Dago." No offence was taken by Enso or by Blue's fellow Councillors.

Angus Blue clashed once with Prime Minister Lester B. (Mike) Pearson, who was at a Legion Atlantic Command convention soft-selling his government's approach to bilingualism and biculturalism.

"Listen, Bye," he told the PM, "if English was good enough for Jesus Christ, it's good enough for us guys down here."

Then, for good measure, he threw in a few profane broadsides.

Ever the diplomat, ever conciliatory, Pearson replied: "We aren't trying to legislate language for anyone. It doesn't matter a whit what language Canadians speak – English, French or the language of the previous speaker." Angus Blue was smart enough to quit when he was behind.

The morning paper the next day carried a photo of Angus Blue wearing his blue blazer and beret, both carrying Legion crests – with his arm around Mike Pearson's shoulder.

The hot stove league that gathered on fine evenings on Senator's Corner in Glace Bay under the chairmanship of "Big Cy" MacDonald was always good for the latest Angus Blue miscue – like the night he went to Vince MacGillivray's funeral parlour wearing his brand new "double-chested suit and Stilson hat" from Hughie MacIntyre's haberdashery.

UGLY KING OF THE SEA

Glace Bay's resident wit, the late "Big Cy" MacDonald, pontificated that the bravest man in the world had to be the man who ate the very first lobster.

"They are ugly little buggers," he would say.

In any beauty contest, the lobster would probably wind up in a dead heat with the skate fish as the ugliest creature to inhabit the ocean.

Gaius Plinius Secundus (Pliny) – AD 23-79 – called them *locusta* (locust) in his 37-volume Historia Naturalis. Aristotle wrote about lobsters in BC 200. They were called *lopstyre* in Old English.

Pliny and Big Cy were both right. The crustacean was an ugly locust-like bugger, indeed, and it must have taken a very brave man to tackle the first one.

Today, the lobster is the undisputed King of the Sea.

TRUE lobsters, Homarus Americanus, are only caught in the cold waters off Maine and along the eastern Atlantic from Labrador to Delaware – a 1,300-mile stretch that includes Cape Breton. Other so-called lobsters – horned lobster, spiny lobster and rock lobster – are found south of the Bay of Biscay to South Africa, North America's Pacific coast and in the south Atlantic off Carolina.

They are also called langouste and scampi, but lobsters they are not. They have no large claws like Homarus Americanus. Instead, they have big, fat spiny tails. Canadian fisheries department efforts to introduce the East Coast lobster to warmer Pacific waters ended in failure.

There is no mistaking Homarus Americanus. It has two strong claws – a big-toothed crusher for crunching food crustaceans and a smaller ripper claw for tearing flesh away from shells.

Cape Bretoners like to tell the story of a Caper who entered one of Toronto's poshest restaurants and ordered the biggest boiled lobster in the house. The waiter reappeared shortly with a three-pounder on a large fishplate.

There was only one problem: the lobster was missing a claw. The Cape Bretoner looked at the lobster and then at the waiter, who said condescendingly: "You see, sir, often they fight in the tank and one will sever the claw of another."

"In that case," replied the Caper, "take this one back and bring me the winner."

ALEXANDER Pope, Lewis Carroll and T. S. Eliot gave the lobster immortality, but recognition and acceptance did not follow. Respectability was a long time coming. When I was growing up in Cape Breton in the 1940s and 1950s, lobster was a few notches down the food chain from dog food. Even poorer families looked down their noses at the lowly crustacean.

Jewish families did not eat lobsters because the "crawlers" were bottom-feeding shellfish that were scavengers and ate other shellfish. The Hebrew religion prohibits fish without scales.

In the 1960s, Senator Mike Forrestall was a political organizer for Premiers Bob Stanfield and Ike Smith. One day Mike and I drove down to the shore to meet the lobster boats coming in. A skipper offered to sell us a dozen live ones for $5. Better still, he'd give us the creatures if we gave him unemployment insurance stamps that were easily purchased at any post office.

Today, lobster fishermen off the Cape Breton coast are in a tax bracket all by themselves. Equipped with a small Cape Island boat and a licence for their zone, they are entitled to lay out 250 pots and fish for two months. There is no limit to the number of lobsters they may catch – only on the number of pots. The only taboo is that if they land a female with visible eggs, they must throw her back in. Some unscrupulous fishermen hold the female up against the boat's exhaust pipe and blow the eggs off.

They check their traps from dawn to dusk and when they return to harbour they are paid as much as $7.00 a pound for their catch. Those same lobsters will fetch $9-11 a pound at market in Saint John, more in Ottawa.

When lobster season ends on one coast, it opens on another, so there is year round lobster fishing. After a season ends for him, a lobster fisherman has an opportunity to participate in a very limited 200,000-pound snow crab season. Snow crabs fetch half as much as landed lobster.

Nova Scotia lobster fishermen grumble that Prince Edward Island fishermen are biting off their noses to spite their faces. The PEI fishers catch 8-12 ounce lobsters, while Nova Scotia boats only keep 14-16 ounce specimens.

It is an old wives tale that lobsters squeal when they are dropped in boiling water. They are incapable of uttering any sound. Another old wives tale is that you never eat lobsters with a dairy product – milk, cream or ice cream. I listened to my mother and have never tempted fate.

Novice lobster eaters often make the mistake of cooking them in boiling fresh water; the result is akin to eating silly putty.

Lobsters must be boiled in seawater or fresh water generously laced with coarse salt. The best lobster is a fresh lobster. Lobsters can survive for several weeks in a tank, but they will not feed in captivity. Gradually, they lose weight and shrink inside their shells.

Seafood restaurants in the Maritimes often squeeze every last bit of flavour out of lobsters. They chop up the shells and freeze them until they are ready to be simmered for fish broth. Then they dry the shells, grind them into flour and use it in lobster bisque soup.

ANOTHER lobster story with whiskers on it is about a couple from "away" – Upper Canadians – who honeymooned at Parlee Beach in Shediac, New Brunswick. The bride was a "Mommy's girl" and Mommy insisted on accompanying the newlyweds on their honeymoon.

One day, Mommy went in for a swim, got caught in a rip tide and was swept out to sea. The Royal Canadian Mounted Police dragged the area for a week, but her body was not found. They abandoned the search and the young newlyweds returned home to pick up their lives.

A week later a telegram arrived from the RCMP with the terse message: HAVE RECOVERED MOTHER IN LAW'S BODY. NINE LOBSTERS ATTACHED TO TOES. PLEASE ADVISE DISPOSITION.

The husband, a former Cape Bretoner, cabled back: SHIP LOBSTERS AND SET HER AGAIN.

ONLY IN GLACE BAY! THE STRANGEST OF PROCESSIONS

Mourners prepared to move off to two different cemeteries after separate funeral services at the same hour at Patten's Funeral Home and V. J. MacGillivray's Funeral Home in Glace Bay. The names of the deceased have been omitted out of respect for the dead, and to frustrate the curious.

Patten's was located on Union Street in the middle of the block. MacGillivray's was located nearby on Reserve Street/ Winnifred Square, the beginning or the end of the main Sydney-Glace Bay highway.

The funeral service at Patten's was for a very popular and well-known member of the Royal Canadian Legion – a Cape Breton Highlander who fought in World War II.

The John Bernard Croak, V.C., Branch of the Canadian Legion was just a few doors down Union Street from Patten's. (Private John Bernard Croak,

Newfoundland born but Glace Bay raised, was awarded the Victoria Cross at Amiens, France, in 1918 during World War I.)

Patten's funeral directors had a premonition that it wasn't going to be an ordinary run-of-the mill funeral, that it wasn't going to come off according to the normal drill.

Some of the Legion brothers had stopped off at the Legion bar for a heart starter – or two. Mike Curry of Curry's Funeral Homes says it was standard practice for the Legion members to meet at the Legion bar for a few bumpers of rum and coke before the funeral service of a fellow Legion member.

The service at Patten's began to unravel when the Legion standard bearer unfurled his banner and raised his pikestaff. The sharp metal spear of the pole pierced a ceiling tile and stuck in it. When he attempted to yank on the staff to free it and seat it in its leather socket, he succeeded in stabbing himself in the groin.

A funeral director who was there said he was lucky – "lucky indeed. Another inch or two and he might have been singing soprano at the graveside."

SIMULTANEOUSLY, the second funeral for an 82 year-old "sweet little old lady" was preparing to move off from MacGillivray's Funeral Home.

The funeral from Patten's could not make a right turn and proceed along Union Street towards Senator's Corner, because a left turn to go up Main Street was prohibited. So the cortege made a left turn onto Union Street and proceeded to Reserve Street where it would make a right turn over the railway tracks.

The railway tracks, formerly the old Sydney and Louisburg (S&L) railway line, ran into Devco's "Big Shops" where equipment for underground mining was serviced and maintained. In better days, it served as a spur line into the coal company's round house for locomotives.

The intersection of Union and Reserve streets was a T-shaped junction. Union Street was the crossbar and Reserve Street was the main spine.

From there, the Patten funeral cortege would proceed up Reserve Street, make a right turn up Victoria Street, follow it to its end and then make a left turn up Main Street to the cemeteries. It was a roundabout route, but the most direct access to Main Street given that a left hand turn was banned at Senator's Corner.

Half of the funeral cortege made it across the tracks before a train came by and blocked the crossing. The first half carried on and proceeded up Victoria Street.

When it was safe to cross the railway tracks, the second half proceeded across. The first thing they saw was the tail end of the MacGillivray funeral procession. So, unknowingly, but naturally, they followed it all the way out to the Forest Haven Memorial Gardens on the Sydney-Glace Bay Highway near the airport.

When the cortege arrived at Forest Haven, scores of Legion members poured out of cars.

A family member commented: "I didn't know auntie was going to be buried in a Legion funeral. Why were all these Legion members gathering at the grave site?"

The Canadian Legion was there in force, dressed in their distinctive crested blue blazers and berets. Even the standard bearer, his wound discreetly dressed and bandaged, stood at respectful attention as pallbearers carried the coffin to the grave.

The officiating clergyman was puzzled, but the show had to go on.

The deceased lady's relatives were at a total loss when a Legion bugler placed his instrument to his lips and played a salute to a fallen warrior – the last post.

One lady was terminally confused until a question came from the mouth of a babe. Her small daughter turned to her and said: "I didn't know Granny was a veteran."

Meanwhile, up on Chapel Hill, a World War II veteran was laid to his final rest without the benefit of the presence of many of his Legion comrades – least of all the bugler and his mournful dirge of the last post, but several miles away, "Auntie" went to her eternal reward with all the pomp and ceremony the Canadian Legion had to offer.

One Glace Bay resident, whose late father owned and operated a popular fruit and vegetable store on Senator's Corner, quipped that "the only thing missing from 'Auntie's' funeral was a volley of rifle fire over the grave and a squadron of RCAF fighter jets flying the Missing Man Formation" overhead.

GENIUS OR HUSTLER?

GUGLIELMO MARCONI

Was Guglielmo Marconi really the father of wireless communication, or was he a hustler who piggy-backed on Nikola Tesla's technology to send signals across the Atlantic at the speed of light? On December 12, 1901, when Marconi sent the world's first wireless signal from Poldhu, Cornwall to Signal Hill in St. John's, Newfoundland, he claimed he had not read reports of Tesla's 1893 experiments.

IN 1895, Marconi introduced his "invention" in London, but scientists say it is the same device Tesla had already described in his research papers. Tesla registered the very first radio patent in 1897. In 1898, Tesla demonstrated a remote-controlled boat in New York protected by patent No. 613809.

In 1900, Tesla told associates he was planning to sue Marconi for patent infringement.

Using £50,000 borrowed from a London bank, Marconi took his experiments to Cape Cod and Signal Hill. The world was impressed when he sent the first trans-Atlantic wireless message, but few if any noticed he was using technology from Tesla's patent.

In 1917, Tesla announced a breakthrough locating metallic objects using radio signals – the birth of radar. In 1943, nine month's after Tesla's death, the U.S. Patent Office ruled that Tesla must be considered the inventor of wireless transmission and radio. Marconi's claims that he was ignorant of Tesla's patents were deemed to be false.

Tesla may have discovered the physics, but it was Marconi who had the daring to pledge everything he owned and borrow £50,000 to build transmitters in Cornwall, England; Clifden, Ireland; St. John's; Cape Cod; and Glace Bay, Nova Scotia.

The road to his first transmission in 1901 was a rocky one. Severe storms blew down his four 213-foot wooden towers at Cape Cod and then, again, in Newfoundland. Marconi was at the end of his resources and finances. The very first signal he received on Signal Hill used kites and balloons to send copper wire aloft.

Discouraged, Marconi had reached the point where he was not able to continue. He decided to return to England. In Sydney, Nova Scotia, where he was to board a boat, he had a chance meeting with Alex Johnston, the Liberal Member of Parliament for Cape Breton. Johnston bulldozed an $80,000 grant from Wilfrid Laurier's government and Marconi was back in business.

Four 213-foot wooden towers were erected at Table Head in Glace Bay. Marconi's grant was contingent on success reports and was paid in instalments. The last instalment was due December 15, 1902, the day Marconi was to send the first west-to-east message to Cornwall.

It was a miserable day – foggy and cold – and the experimental equipment was untried. If Marconi failed, the final portion of his grant would not be paid. Cape Breton's most distinguished historian, Albert Almon, alleges the experiment failed. The message could not be sent, so Marconi faked the results and lived to succeed another day – and claim his final payment.

BEFORE his experiments in Canada, Marconi had succeeded in sending wireless signals 3.5 miles across the Bristol Channel. Next he transmitted 31 miles across the channel to France and then 196 miles from the Isle of Wight to The Lizard, Cornwall. Scientists believed the range of wireless transmission was only 200 miles because of the earth's curvature.

Marconi had the luck of the Irish. Though he was born in Italy of an Italian father, his mother was Irish. Annie Jameson was a member of the wealthy Jameson whisky distilling family.

In 1910, Marconi's newfangled invention received an enormous leg up when wireless was used on the high seas to apprehend a suspected murderer. Dr. Hawley Harvey Crippen, a fifty year-old American dentist living in London, poisoned his wife, dismembered her body, burned her bones in a furnace and buried wrapped parcels of her flesh in his basement.

Suspicious neighbours alerted Scotland Yard and a team of forensic technicians found Crippen's wife's remains. By this time, Crippen and his mistress, Ethel LeNeve, were on board Canadian Pacific's *Montrose* bound for Montreal. LeNeve was disguised as a boy – Crippen's "son."

Montrose's Captain, H. G. Kendall, recognized Crippen from wanted photos in newspapers and he instructed his wireless operator to alert Scotland Yard that he was on board. Inspector Walter Dew raced to Liverpool, boarded a faster White Star liner, *Laurentic*, which would reach Montreal before *Montrose*. Inspector Dew left *Laurentic* at Father Point, Quebec and boarded *Montrose* disguised as a harbour pilot.

Crippen was arrested, returned to England and hanged after a sensational murder trial. Ethel LeNeve was tried and acquitted after a brilliant defence by F. E. Smith, later Lord Birkenhead. She did not "take the box" to testify. The jury deliberated only twenty minutes before bringing in a not guilty verdict.

After the trial, the Lord Chief Justice told Smith he should have put her on the stand to testify on her own behalf. F. E.'s reply was: "No, my lord, I knew what she would say. You did not."

Ethel LeNeve vanished after the trial and was never heard from again.

The murder, the high seas drama, the arrest and lurid trial gave instant credibility that Marconi's wireless communication was an idea whose time had come.

Another beneficiary of the Crippen case was the British mystery writer, Edgar Wallace. Dr. Crippen was reading *Four Just Men* on the voyage and often discussed the book with the captain. When this snippet of news was sent to London by wireless, it made Edgar Wallace's name as famous as Crippen's all over Europe.

IN 1912, the Marconi family planned a trip to New York by ship. Marconi's plans changed and he was forced to depart earlier on a faster ship. His wife and daughter also cancelled their original reservations and remained in England. Outside their home in Southampton, they waved to passengers on the ship they should have taken as it cruised by. It was *Titanic*.

When *Titanic* struck an iceberg in April, 1912 Marconi's wireless played a key role in saving hundreds of lives by directing rescue ships to the scene of the disaster. The wireless operator at Cape Race, Newfoundland stayed at his post 96 hours. He flashed out the names and addresses of survivors to the world and anxious relatives.

GUGLIELMO Marconi shared the Nobel prize for physics in 1909 even though a radio pioneer, Alexandr Popov, told a congress of electrical engineers: "The emission and reception of signals by Marconi is nothing new. In America, the famous engineer, Nikola Tesla, carried the same experiments in 1893." Tesla publicly said he would refuse a Nobel prize if it was offered. It was more important to him to see his name on each of his inventions. For that, he would give a Nobel prize away.

Britain minted a special £2 coin honouring Marconi. On May 11, 2001, Canada Post issued a Tourist Attractions stamp depicting Signal Hill. In 1974, Marconi was commemorated by an 8¢

stamp on the 100th anniversary of his birth. Canadian and British mints issued joint commemorative coin sets.

A very small Parks Canada museum dedicated to Marconi now stands on the Table Head site in Glace Bay. It is little advertised and poorly signed. Even though admission is free, few people visit it.

When Marconi died in 1937, he was accorded a rare and still unique honour: every radio station in the world was silent for two minutes.

REMEMBERING CHRISTMAS

Growing up in the coal mining town of Glace Bay during World War II was a hardscrabble experience but, though money was scarce, Christmas was special.

It was special because my parents made sacrifices and our parish, St. Anne's, taught us the spiritual meaning of Christmas.

Christmas is a major celebration in the Catholic Church calendar. It is a reminder of the birth of Jesus in a manger in Bethlehem. The celebration of Christ's birth, Christmas, shepherds and the Magi are tenets of my Faith.

In his essay on Liberty, John Stuart Mill wrote that every man has the right to go to hell in the manner of his own choosing, so long as he doesn't bother his neighbour. If others choose not to espouse the Christian Christmas that is their choice. Just don't deny others and me the right to believe in them and celebrate them our way each year.

POVERTY is a great leveller and therefore Glace Bay was a role model for brotherly love and religious tolerance. Jews and Christians, Catholics and Protestants, worked and lived side by side in harmony. Immigrants from Scotland, Wales, England, the British colony of Newfoundland, the Ukraine, Poland, the Baltic republics, Greece and China built the town and made it a good place to live. EVEN back in the 1940s, commercial interests sought to downplay Christmas by substituting "Xmas" for Christmas. It caused an uproar. Clergy and laity alike recoiled against this unacceptable rebuff and launched a counter campaign to "Bring back Christ to Christmas."

No Christmas is complete without a decorated evergreen tree. My Da, my brother and I would go into the nearby woods with a hatchet and chop one down. So did everybody else in town. We never questioned whose land it was – the coal company's or the Crown's – and nobody ever confronted us. If it were a crime, everybody in Glace Bay would have spent Christmas in the local crowbar hotel.

My Da was a virtuoso, felling a tree and decorating it with fragile coloured bulbs, glass peacocks with long silken plumes for tails, coloured lights, tinsel and angel hair. One Christmas he stepped back to admire his handiwork and he saw the spruce coming at him to do a face plant. Boots, the family cat, had climbed up the trunk. I can recall my Da's exact Gaelic, and they weren't words one would hear in church.

The focal point of Christmas was Midnight Mass. St. Anne's, with twin wooden Norman-type steeples, was the largest wooden church in all of Canada. It burned to the ground during a wild winter storm in the late 1980s.

The interior of the church was the finest tribute to God working class parishioners could render. A massive Casavant Freres pipe organ had about 4,000 pipes, and the wooden church shook when an organist turned it loose.

The area around the altar was as if sculpted out of a single block of oak. The Communion rail was a combination of local marble and pewter. The Stations of the Cross were genuine oil paintings in the Renaissance style.

There wasn't much time spent in classrooms the week before Christmas.

The nuns, the Halifax-based Sisters of Charity, spent hours drilling altar boys and choirboys with the sadism of parade square drill sergeants.

The spacing for processions down an aisle was "a pew apart." Sisters Marion James and Mary Doris never knew why we all giggled or wore broad smiles. They couldn't hear "Web" MacIsaac mumbling "phew a fart, phew a fart."

Altar boys wore black soutanes/ cassocks and highly starched white surplices. Choirboys wore scarlet cassocks. They also had neat red capes. Kids like me from coal company families wore plain white cotton surplices. Kids whose Das owned small businesses or who were professionals might have six inches of crocheted lace attached to the bottom of their surplices.

St. Anne's had no need for seraphim and cherubim. There were 75-80 freshly-scrubbed angels in the choir or on the sides of the altar. Every one of them had a new 35¢ haircut from Bob MacKenzie's, Iggy Routledge's or Joe MacKinnon's barber shops. No one would believe that an hour earlier they were pounding the hell out of one another and throwing slippers in the changing room.

Christmas Eve was as close to magic as one could get. The altar was ablaze with candles. The powerful, natural tenor voices of George Walker and Calder Steele boomed out "Ave Maria," "Adeste Fideles" and "Panis Angelicus" and the forty-boy choir contributed "Silent Night," "When Blossoms Flowered Mid the Snows" and "O Little Town of Bethlehem."

The lead soloist, Bernie MacMullin, had a rich soprano voice that would give Charlotte Church a run for her money. I haven't laid eyes on Bernie for more than fifty years, but I hope, for his sake, his voice changed.

Midnight Mass for ten to twelve year-old boys was a rite of passage, a Catholic version of a Hebrew bar mitzvah. You reached manhood if you managed to survive the long service without fainting or falling asleep in the overheated church. Most of us made it, but those who didn't brought scorn and derision upon themselves.

After Mass, my parents, my brother and I walked the half-mile home to a warm kitchen. There, my mother unleashed a feast worthy of a Roman emperor –home made oyster stew, a whole baked ham served cold, home made green tomato chow, home made pickles, freshly baked bread, Parkerhouse rolls, shortbread, dark and light fruitcake and my Da's favourite, *bonnach* (Scots soda bread) – washed down with quarts of Cape Breton's national drink – strongly brewed loose tea.

Could life possibly be better anywhere?

Then we hung our stockings – usually a clean pit sock – on the mantle. The next morning, we'd find our stocking filled with a couple of walnuts and pecans, humbugs, jaw breakers, a silver dollar, always a religious medal and a wartime luxury: an orange.

I saw my very first banana two or three years after the war ended. A corner grocer, Bert Rankin, had a stalk hanging in his store and it became a tourist attraction – the eighth wonder of the world.

I paid a visit to our two-holer outhouse before I was sent off to the warm bed I shared with "Boots," or I should say Boots allowed me to share with him. My Da told us Santa Claus wouldn't come down the chimney until we were asleep.

One of my school chums, Lonnie Bourgeois, became an instant hero when he told us all he hid, waited up and saw Santa. We all believed him. I wanted a piece of Lonnie's immortality, so I tried to stay up one Christmas. But I fell asleep behind the chesterfield and missed him.

The next morning – more magic under the tree: maybe a hockey stick, a new pair of skates, hand-knitted wool socks and mitts, books by Robert Louis Stevenson, a dynamite toy that was designed and built to last forever, a Red Ryder BB rifle, a Gilbert chemistry set, a Meccano Erector set or a Lionel model train. In the excitement of tearing open our presents, we failed to realize there was very little under the tree for Ma and Da.

MY boyhood years were sheer magic – love, warmth, sharing, enjoying the mysteries of my faith and the pomp and ceremony of Midnight Mass.

Every Christmas since, I like to sit in front of our own brightly lit balsam tree with all the house lights out. I think of the powerful words T. S. Eliot penned for Archbishop Thomas Becket's riveting Christmas Day sermon in the play *Murder in the Cathedral.*

"We both rejoice and mourn at once and for the same reason. For either joy will be overcome by mourning, or mourning will be cast out by joy; so it is only in these our Christian mysteries that we can rejoice and mourn at once for the same reason."

Ma and Da – John Angus (Jack) MacAdam and Ellen Johanna (Nellie) Gallivan – have been gone for more than thirty years and I mourn their passing. But I can rejoice for the years I had with them and thank them for the start in life they gave me.

SATURDAYS AT THE SAVOY

Growing up in Glace Bay, the old Savoy Theatre was the pot of gold at the end of the week. We collected beer bottles, pop bottles and pieces of scrap metal from roadside ditches and sold them to Goldman's on Reserve Street to raise the 12¢ we needed for Saturday's matinee.

Looking back, we certainly got our money's worth. For 12¢ we saw trailers of coming attractions, a newsreel, a cartoon, a cliff-hanger serial like *Fu Manchu*, the *Lone Ranger* or *Zorro*, and a double feature. The double feature was usually back-to-back dusters such as *Hopalong Cassidy*, the *Durango Kid* or *Roy Rogers and Trigger* or *Gene Autry and Champion*.

Some of us took our cap guns to the show and blazed away at the guys in the black hats on the screen – Hoppy needed all the help he could get despatching a superior force of 20-30 outlaws to Boot Hill. We never stopped to question how

Hopalong's six-shooter came to have an endless supply of .45 bullets.

We saw so many Westerns my best friend, "Web" MacIsaac, used to say he was sure Johnny Mack Brown must have a room above the Savoy.

The Savoy was owned by the Connors family, and Edgar Connors was the manager. During World War II, the Savoy sponsored patriotic drives collecting aluminum pots, empty metal toothpaste tubes and fat drippings. The metal was used in the manufacture of Spitfire and Hurricane fighter planes. The fat was used to make soap and ammunition. If you brought a contribution, the 12¢ admission fee was waived.

Mothers guarded their aluminum kitchen cookware zealously.

Edgar Connors had a sign done up professionally for the lobby. It read: "Ladies, Leave Your Fat Cans Here." We all thought it was quite raunchy. Knowing Edgar, the double entendre was probably intentional, but the sign survived the entire war.

Altar boy and choir boy practices were scheduled by Father Hank Nash and Steve MacGillivray, so we'd be able to get to the Savoy on time. We'd gallop down Main Street, cross over the railway tracks, cut through coal company property and race across Union Street to the Savoy.

One wintry Saturday afternoon, during a blizzard, tragedy struck. Our twelve year-old pal Terry Donovan didn't look either way. His glasses were steamed up and his peripheral vision was blocked by his parka hood. The Glace Bay-Sydney bus couldn't stop on the icy street and Terry was killed instantly when he was crushed up against a telephone pole.

WHEN the house lights went out at the Savoy, so did Edgar. He headed down the street to Steve Markadonis' poolroom or next door to the upstairs Casino billiard emporium. Edgar was one of the coolest pool shots in town and the regular Saturday afternoon and evening money games of "Life" and "Pill" fattened his weekly take home pay.

When Edgar was losing, which wasn't often, it was unwise to rub it in. His sense of humour vanished when he was off his game. He was so wedded to the almighty dollar, we used to say that he'd skin a flea for the tallow.

He left good order and discipline to his usher, Gordie Roberts. Gordie was always booted and spurred in a blue uniform with red lapels and a red stripe down the pants legs. Come to think of it, I never saw Gordie in any threads other than his usher's outfit. I swear to God that I recently saw a lady wearing an identical designer outfit by Escada, and it probably set her back about a thousand bucks.

Armed with a flashlight, Gordie prowled the aisles looking for kids who didn't want to miss any of the show and peed on the back of the seat in front of them instead of going to the washroom.

Edgar had a reputation as the town wit. Always resplendent in a double breasted Glen Check suit, shirt and tie, he was looked up to because he was probably the first person in Glace Bay to fly Trans Canada Airway's North Star prop plane from Sydney to Halifax.

When the plane landed, passengers walked 100 feet or so to the terminal. En route, they had to run a gauntlet of liveried limousine drivers flogging free limo service to downtown Halifax, if you would stay at their hotel.

All along the tarmac one would hear "Lord Nelson?" "Nova Scotian?" "Dresden Arms?"

Edgar felt a hand tugging at his sleeve asking: "Lord Nelson, Halifax?"

His reply: "No, Edgar Connors, Glace Bay!"

THE very last time I set foot inside the Savoy was in 1951 when I graduated from St. Anne's High School and received my diploma on stage from town school supervisor O. B. Smith. The boys all wore white pants, a black jacket and black bow tie. We marched out to the recessional strains of Mendelssohn's "War March of the Priests."

I was the proudest kid in the Bay. My father and mother, Jack and Nell, were in the audience and positively beamed. I had graduated from high school, finished first in my class and was a leading candidate for the $250 Knights of Columbus scholarship to St. FX.

I was awakened from my day dream by someone pulling on my sleeve. It was Edgar Connors. Naturally, I assumed he wanted to pay homage to St. Anne's leading scholar. But, no! He said: "Run home and get changed and I'll beat you a couple of games of snooker in the KOC rooms – 25¢ a game."

I took him for 75¢ and quit while I was ahead, before he "accidentally" poked me with his designer pool cue – the one with the black ebony and mother of pearl hand grip. That was just after I had had the stupidity to say to him: "Edgar, if I keep playing 'Fish' like you, I probably won't need the KOC scholarship."

WHEN POLITICS WERE SERIOUS FUN

Once upon a time, being involved in politics was personal – and fun.

If you were a MacAdam in Glace Bay, three things were certain. You were a Scot, a Catholic and a Conservative, and not necessarily in that order. A mixed marriage was when a Conservative married a Liberal.

I had a first cousin, Donald, who was christened Donald Arthur Meighen MacAdam. How's that for wearing your political stripe on your Baptismal sleeve?

The major parties' core vote in small town Nova Scotia was as predictable and regular as Exlax.

In one provincial riding – Hants County – more often than not, the election ended in a dead heat and the returning officer had to cast the deciding vote. One election was voided by Nova Scotia's Supreme Court.

The Tory and Liberal candidates were Vern and Ernie, and even they didn't take themselves seriously. They campaigned on the slogans "It's Vern's Turn" or "It's Ern's Turn."

Our member of parliament in Cape Breton South was CCFer Clarie Gillis. Clarie could have won the riding running on a laundry ticket, because he was "one of us" – a tough, blunt-speaking former coal miner.

Clarie was first elected in 1940 and served in the Commons until he was trounced by Diefenbaker candidate, Donald MacInnis (by 3,355 votes) in 1957.

Tom Van Dusen, Sr., was a reporter with the *Ottawa Journal* and remembers "sitting up all night, holding Clarie's hand" the night Clarie punched out a waiter in the old Windsor Tavern on Queen Street in Ottawa.

Clarie was afraid the altercation would "make the papers." It did. Clarie was page one news. The fallout: he was re-elected with an increased majority. Now, if he had lost the fight with the waiter he decked....

Then there was the case of the Liberal candidate in the Maritimes who lost two consecutive federal elections and a by-election. His supporters accused the Tories of smear tactics – "dirty tricks." Liberals believed that Conservatives were behind the nasty whispering campaign that their man had stopped drinking.

When an election writ was dropped, the first order of business was to dispatch fast cutters to the French islands of St. Pierre et Miquelon, off Newfoundland. Their return cargo was kegs of dark rum that would be decanted into 12-ounce "mickeys."

The going rate to sway a doubtful voter was $2 or a mickey of rum. Over in Prince Edward Island, the tariff was a mickey or a "yard of shore gravel" for a driveway.

In the late 1940s and early 1950s, Bob Stanfield was leader of Nova Scotia's Opposition Conservative rump. His constant travelling companion was Don Haggart, the party's only paid organizer. Haggart was probably the last man in Nova Scotia to wear gray spats.

Part of Nova Scotia's folklore, perhaps apocryphal, is how the pair campaigned in Halifax County's Black communities. There were 32,000 Blacks in all of Canada and half lived in enclaves in Africville in Halifax or in outlying crossroads hamlets.

While Stanfield made his pitch, Don would be on his knees wielding a tape measure. The bewildered prospect who was being courted would become increasingly nervous, until Haggart explained: "I am measuring you for a uniform, and if we win the election you can count on a job as a porter on the CNR."

In 1956, Stanfield turned out a tired Liberal government that had been entrenched for 23 years. The Liberal Party had been rent asunder by bitter, internal religious infighting over a successor to the unbeatable Catholic premier, the late Angus L. Macdonald, who died in office.

Outside his safe seat in Inverness County, the most feared Liberal cabinet minister was Attorney General Malcolm Patterson. Surprisingly, he went down to personal defeat in 1956.

Two Antigonish Tories, one who later became mayor and the other a provincial magistrate, celebrated Stanfield's victory and Malcolm Patterson's defeat by going on a week-long "toot."

Every day for a week, they sent Malcolm the same telegram: "WE'RE GLAD YOU LOST, YOU SON OF A BITCH."

Running a campaign was the preserve of adults. Youngsters, such as yours truly, were not wanted on the voyage and were not welcome in a candidate's committee rooms.

The men scrubbed coal dust away after work, dressed in their Sunday best, stood around the committee rooms, trying to look wise, and pontificated about current events and world affairs.

There was never any liquor in the committee rooms, but the tea was strong enough to stun a tapeworm.

The ladies seized the day to trot out their finest frocks and hats while they addressed and stuffed envelopes. Kids weren't even wanted as delivery boys, because first class postage and bulk mail rates were so cheap.

Television was still a few years down the road. Pamphlets, picnics and candidates meetings were the main campaign vehicles. All-candidates meetings and debates were unheard of.

Political meetings were more fun than the proverbial barrel of monkeys, and leather-lunged hecklers had ample opportunity to polish their routines. How a candidate parried their barbs could determine the result of an election.

If a candidate was slow on rebuttal, he was adjudged as "not being too swift" and, therefore, unworthy of support.

Private automobiles with loudspeakers mounted on the roof prowled neighbourhoods blaring out party gospel.

The visit by a national party leader was front page news, and meeting halls would be jam-packed with partisan supporters.

Campaigns were hands-on situations. Voters could actually meet and talk to candidates. They did not appear in living rooms on the other side of a TV camera lens. They were not insulated by spin doctors and would-be kingmakers.

All that changed forever in the campaigns of 1957 and 1958, when John Diefenbaker mesmerized a nation with his hypnotic TV presence. More and more, politics became the preserve of the huckster. Less and less, they were contests between in-the-flesh and in-your-face personalities.

Television could be configured to make a sow's ear look like a silk purse. A candidate with the charisma of a speed bump and the IQ of a telephone pole could be portrayed as an articulate spokesman for his party – thanks to the sleight of hand and eye of a gifted film or videotape editor.

The medium did indeed become the message. I often wonder how giants like Angus L. Macdonald, Louis St. Laurent, Mackenzie King, Leslie Frost, Arthur Meighen, Tommy Douglas and M. J. Coldwell would fare today.

My guess is they would come across as being so stodgy they would have difficulty winning their own parties' nominations.

There is an actual case history of an Ottawa Tory candidate whose handlers commissioned a firm of professional image makers. The consultants were asked to come up with a campaign strategy.

Their advice – sound, as it turned out to be – was to keep the candidate under wraps. Every time he surfaced or made a statement, he lost votes. He surfaced too often and did and said too many dumb things that he lost while his party formed a government.

In the United States, a candidate who received a Democratic nomination for Congress was agitated because he had no campaign office, no workers and no communication with the Democratic National Committee.

Jim Farley, Franklin D. Roosevelt's campaign manager, took the man down to the New York docks. The Queen Mary was preparing to enter harbour.

Farley said: "See that big liner?"

"Yes!"

"Well then, what's that following her in her wake?"

"Flotsam and jetsam – garbage!"

"Right you are! FDR is your liner, so go home and stop worrying."

And so he did, and so he won his election.

THE MEN OF THE DEEPS

The Men of the Deeps – North America's only group of singing coal miners – were a happy afterthought in 1966. The late Nina Cohen, the catalyst behind a miners' museum as a 1967 Centennial project, thought it appropriate to add a choir for the opening.

Cape Breton does not share the rich tradition of choral singing, as in Wales's valleys and villages. Churches in industrial Cape Breton had amateur choirs directed by amateurs. There were a few barber shop quartets and a small pool of talented but untrained soloist singers.

Nina was the wife of a prosperous Sydney businessman and she was a tireless local tourism booster.

She approached professional Glace Bay musician and choir director, Steve MacGillivray, for help. She also recruited prominent folklore researcher Dr. Helen Creighton and the late Ann Terry MacLellan.

Terry was a much-loved Sydney radio and TV personality with a huge listening audience. Her stage name was "Ann Terry." She left broadcasting abruptly to head up Cape Breton Development Corporation's public affairs department. Choir organizers turned to DEVCO for start-up funding. The money was forthcoming.

Moosehead Breweries sponsored the miners' choir in a Halifax television production. A series of debut concerts in the Fall of 1966 sold out.

The group's midwives agonized over a name. One of the first suggested was "The Miners' Chorus." Others suggested were "Men of the Slopes" and "Men of the Shafts." Finally, they settled on "Men of the Deeps."

Nina and Dr. Creighton persuaded a young St. Francis Xavier University music professor, Jack O'Donnell, to ready the chorus for local concerts and a world debut at Expo 67.

Jack had left his hometown of Portland, Maine, in 1954 to enroll at St. FX. Except for sabbaticals at Gonzaga University, Spokane and King's College, London, he never left Antigonish. He married a college classmate, Judy McGrath from St. John's, Newfoundland.

He was a strange choice to direct a choir of 28 tough, uneducated coal miners. He was trained in classical piano. His post-graduate work was in 18th-century liturgical music.

Nevertheless, for the next 36 years he made the 485 kilometre round trip to Glace Bay every Sunday for rehearsals. He blended resonant four-part singing – first tenors, second tenors, baritones and basses – with the distinctive Cape Breton folk sound.

Jack logged more than 900,000 kilometres just to conduct rehearsals. His modest stipend barely covered gas and oil.

He has criss-crossed Canada and the United States several times with the singing miners. He was with them when they toured China in 1976 and Kosovo, Yugoslavia, in 1999.

Vanessa Redgrave was filming in Cape Breton and heard The Men of the Deeps sing at an outdoor concert. On the spot, she invited them to participate in benefit concerts for the United Nations Children's Fund in Kosovo. There, they shared a stage with Mikhail Baryshnikov, Elton John, Bruce Cockburn, Lebo M of *Lion King* fame, Phillip Glass, U-2's Bono, Big Country and the Martha Graham Dance Company.

China's second invitation to a Canadian musical group was extended to The Canadian Brass ensemble – The first was Men of the Deeps. They sang "O Canada" on the Great Wall of China.

"There were lumps in our throats and tears were rolling down out cheeks. We were soft-hearted Canadians who had come to realize the value of living in a free country," one chorus member reported.

Everywhere they went, they stopped traffic when their bus was surrounded by thousands of Chinese fans.

They sang at a Blue Jays game. They wowed delegates at United Mine Workers conventions in Denver and Cincinnati. They made TV specials and toured with Rita MacNeil. They were mystery guests on Front Page Challenge.

They backed up folksinger Roger Whittaker on a CD and appeared on two network TV specials with Anne Murray, on CBS and CTV. They sang at nationally televised East Coast Music and Juno awards. They appeared with the RCMP Concert Band at Expo 86, in Vancouver. They sang before 57,000 people in Ottawa on Canada Day.

The late Queen Mother attended two of their concerts and pronounced them "fabulous."

They have been subjects of three National Film Board of Canada productions.

They have recorded four LPs and three CDs. A fourth CD is in progress.

The Province of Nova Scotia saluted them as Ambassadors of the Year.

Jack was awarded the Order of Canada in 1983.

In 1993, University College of Cape Breton (now Cape Breton University) awarded Jack an honorary degree. In 2000, UCCB took the unprecedented step of awarding an honorary degree to the entire 28-man group. Singer "Yogi" Muise jokes that receiving honorary doctorates hasn't gone to their heads: "We aren't real doctors; we can only prescribe M&Ms and moonshine."

THE Men of the Deeps have a signature entrance at concerts. The theatre is plunged in darkness. Dressed in blue coveralls, black T-shirts underneath, wearing steel-capped boots, they form two lines and make their way to the stage from the rear of the hall. The only illumination is from the lamps on their hard-hat helmets.

Occasionally, during a concert, Billy MacPherson and Johnny MacLeod may do an impromptu step dance. Fred Gillis says: "Billy was told he looks like a duck stamping out a grassfire."

There are five original members left in the group. The group's ages range from late 30s to upper 70s. Nina Cohen, Helen Creighton, Anne Murray and Rita MacNeil are Honorary Men of the Deeps.

They performed in sold-out concerts every Tuesday night, all summer long, at the Glace Bay Miners Museum. Locals say it is easier to get a ticket to the Montreal Forum.

In Sydney, Jack O'Donnell was honoured at a $125 a plate testimonial dinner attended by 250. The late Halifax businessman Charlie Keating, Senator Al Graham and local MP Roger Cuzner were the main speakers. The dinner raised $22,000 for the Miners' Museum fundraising campaign.

The hall was sold out just as The Men of the Deeps have sold out Massey Hall, the National Arts Centre, Ottawa's Congress Centre, O'Keefe Centre, Charlottetown's Confederation Centre, Windsor's Chrysler Theatre and stages in scores of small towns across Canada.

Looking back, Jack says his proudest moment came when the group was invited to Nicky Goldschmidt's International Choral Festival, the prestigious month-long festival of the world's finest chorales in Roy Thomson Hall.

Today, Jack is probably the ranking world expert on coal mining songs.

Musicologists say he has the world's largest collection. In 1975, Waterloo Music Company published his "The Men of The Deeps Songbook." A second book, "And Now the Fields are Green" followed, from CBU Press.

Jack and his group perform for the love of music. They earn no salaries whatsoever. One singer says: "It costs me money to belong to this outfit." Their fees barely cover expenses. Their transportation to and from China cost $75,000. They were helped by miners at Lingan and No. 26 collieries, who donated a percentage of their wages through the payroll "check off."

From his home in St. Andrew's, near Antigonish, Jack said: "there isn't much money left over from box office receipts when you have to pay travel, hotel and meal expenses for 32 people."

Money isn't a consideration as long as they can continue to bring their music to the people at affordable ticket prices.

Why do they do it? Wally MacAulay sums it up best: "Yeah, I played Roy Thomson Hall. Not many of us in Cape Breton can say that."

PROPER AND FITTING TRIBUTE

I have always admired the Scots and the Brits for their panache in selecting subjects for their statues and busts in public areas. There are the usual tributes in bronze to deceased monarchs and military leaders. But some of the other selections are surprising and delightful.

In 1911, playwright J. M. Barrie erected a statue of Peter Pan in Kensington Gardens. He did it in the middle of the night so that people would think it had appeared by magic. In 1925, Newfoundland businessman Sir Edgar Bowring asked Peter Pan's sculptor, Sir George Frampton, to cast a twin for Bowring Park in St. John's.

This statue of Peter Pan was in memory of Betty Munn, Sir Edgar's godchild, who drowned along with 100 others when SS *Florizel*, en route to New York, went aground on a reef near Cappahaydn.

In later years, replicas of Sir George's statue of Peter Pan were unveiled in Brussels, Melbourne and Toronto.

The most impressive statue in Bowring Park is of Newfoundland's national animal, the caribou. It commemorates the Royal Newfoundland Regiment. On July 1, 1916, all but 68 members of the Regiment were wiped out at Beaumont Hamel, on the Somme, in a foolhardy charge ordered by British commanders.

Nearby is the statue of the "Fighting Newfoundlander," a sculpture of a Royal Newfoundland Regiment soldier about to throw a hand grenade. Thomas Pittman, a surviving corporal in the "Blue Puttees," posed for the statue.

"Humber," the pet dog of Newfoundland Premier Sir Richard Squires, is also immortalized with a memorial in Bowring Park.

IN Leicester Square, London, near the discount theatre ticket kiosk, there is a statue of Charlie Chaplin in his *Little Tramp* costume.

Near the Canadian High Commission in Trafalgar Square, there is a heroic statue of Edith Cavell, the British nurse who was shot as a spy by a German firing squad in World War I.

Wolfgang Amadeus Mozart lived in London when he was four years old. There is a statue of a four-year old Mozart in Pimlico.

In 1858, a man named John Gray was buried in Greyfriars Churchyard in Edinburgh. For the next fourteen years, his Skye Terrier "Bobby" sneaked into the graveyard and slept on his master's grave every night no matter how rough the weather. During the days, he could be seen in or about the churchyard.

Baroness Burdett Coutts rewarded Bobby's loyalty by commissioning a statue of "Greyfriars Bobby" and a fountain. Bobby is now a major tourist attraction in downtown Edinburgh.

Ottawa, where I have lived for more than forty years, is not known for boldness in remembering our greats and near greats. The exceptions are downtown, near Parliament Hill, where there is a life-size bronze of Terry Fox. Across the street is a small statue of Sir Galahad. It was commissioned privately by Prime Minister Mackenzie King to honour a friend who lost his life in a water rescue attempt.

A couple of blocks east, the Dominion archivist showed some originality by installing a statue of a seated figure on the lawn. The seated figure was of none other than the Dominion archivist himself.

Elsewhere, there is a bland melange of statuary of former prime ministers, one of Samuel de Champlain and one dedicated to a soldier of the Boer War.

On Sapper's Bridge over the Rideau Canal, close to the Chateau Laurier Hotel, there are six empty plinths awaiting occupants. A committee was formed to recommend six names of worthies. As expected, their final choices were bland and uninspiring.

Names like Victoria Cross winners "Smokey" Smith, Cece Merritt, Paul Triquet, Andrew Mynarski and Billy Bishop didn't even make the short list. Dr. Norman Bethune, the surgeon who pioneered mobile blood transfusions, was probably blackballed because he was on the wrong side in the Spanish Civil War and marched with Chinese communist leader Mao Tse Tung. Their deliberations drove home the classic definition of a camel to me — a horse put together by a committee.

In the end, the federal government put the kibosh on the selections and the project is on hold.

IF I were the Lord High Minister Without Portfolio In Charge of Statues, I would heed Joe Howe's advice of August 31, 1871. He told a Howe family reunion: "A wise nation preserves its records, gathers up its muniments, decorates the tombs of its illustrious dead, repairs its great public structures, and fosters national pride and love of country, by perpetual reference to the sacrifices and glories of the past."

Under my stewardship there would be statues or busts of "Big Cy" MacDonald and Angus "Blue" MacDonald on Senator's Corner. "Hughie and Allan" would loom large in bronze along the Esplanade in Sydney. Gussie MacLellan would be cast in bronze outside one of the venues in Glace Bay, or Sydney, where he promoted fights. Judge A. B. MacGillivray would tower large over the entrance to Glace Bay's old Stipendiary Magistrate's Court in the Town Hall.

George "Rockabye" Ross, J. B. "Kid" Adshade, Joe Pyle, "Tommy Gun" Spencer and Mickey MacIntyre would be sculpted in their boxing ring togs.

Hugh MacLennan, Nathan Cohen, Hollywood film director Dan Petrie, the world's fastest human Clarie Demont (100-yard dash world record setter), the Glace Bay Caledonias rugby team, Brother Mathias from Bridgeport (Babe Ruth's mentor), Danny Gallivan, Monsignor M. M. Coady, Angus L. Macdonald, Dr. "Duke" MacIsaac, Leo McIntyre, "Ann Terry" MacLellan and Winston Fitzgerald would be among the first few I would fast-track for statues or busts.

After all, these were the people who contributed most to our quality of life.